HowardGambrillClark.com

Revolt Against Al-Qa`ida

Howard Gambrill Clark

Light of New Orleans Publishing

Manufactured in the United States of America

Cover design by C. Eichler.
Cover illustration by M. Samra to represent the Southwest Asia militias independently fighting the Taliban
and al-Qa`ida.

The views expressed in this publication are the author's
and do not imply endorsement by any U.S. Government
agency. He is writing this book as an independent
citizen. Nothing in this book represents the views,
findings, or conclusions of the U.S. or any other
government or government-affiliated organization.

Library of Congress Cataloging-in-Publication Data

Clark, Howard, 1978-
 Revolt against Al-Qa'ida / by Howard Clark.
    p. cm.
 Includes bibliographical references.
 ISBN 978-0-9827767-0-4 (alk. paper)
 1. Qaida (Organization) 2. Terrorism and mass media. I. Title.
 HV6432.5.Q2C53 2009
 363.325'16--dc22

                    2010025898

In memory of...

Captain John W. Maloney (U.S. Marine Corps), Major General William E. Odom (U.S. Army), Dr. H. Bradford Westerfield, Watkins R. Reckless

...without your professional mentorship, personal counsel, and inspiration, this book and informed efforts to defeat transnational insurrection would not be possible. Your wisdom and courage will live on through your teachings and actions. I will not let you down.

A special thank you to...

The Honorable Charles E. Allen, Major James "Doc" Templin (U.S. Army Special Forces), Dr. Bassam Frangieh, Dr. Hassan Abbas, Brian A. Marcus, Albar Sheikh, M. Javed Ali, Master Gunnery Sergeant Stephen A. Gould (U.S. Marine Corps), Master Sergeant Jason Dale Epperson (U.S. Air Force, Retired), Major Sean P. Daly (U.S. Marine Corps), Ben Fitzgerald

...your guidance and wisdom made this policy proposal possible.

All the author's profits from this book will be sent to Afghan Health & Development Services (www.ahds.org).

Afghan Health & Development Services helps to rehabilitate its country's health infrastructure. Founded by Afghans, this non-profit, non-governmental, non-political organization trains medical staff and provides comprehensive primary health care services to those in need.

CONTENTS

PREFACE

Diesel fumes had become as much a part of life as air and water. The smell no longer fazed me, nor did the 130-degree shade I left behind as I walked across the Marine camp in 2005, naked but for the hand towel clasped around my waist with one hand. As I approached the servants' quarters of Saddam's Ramadi palace for my last shower of my last deployment in Iraq, questions flooded my mind, not the usual ones on tactics, but ones about my impact there. It seemed that our very presence was causing many of the attacks and giving locals a reason to actively or passively support terrorists. Furthermore, we were running after our own tails. My last unit would hop from one town to another, back to the first again and again killing insurgents, but getting nowhere. The insurgents kept coming unabated.

Then a hole opened in the earth in front of me. Dust plumed into the air as I remembered the whistling sound a split second earlier, weak as an afterthought now. I peered into the hole, into what remained of the butt end of a 122-millimeter rocket round, the type insurgents loved to fire from across the river.

Huh.

An EOD team rushed up.

"Think it's a dud," I said, realizing I had not turned into a pink mist.

I took my shower and soon after left the Marines. I was as far away as ever from my personal goal to end al-Qa`ida, not to kill militant after militant or check its ability to attack temporarily, but to permanently end al-Qa`ida.

On the morning of 11 September 2001, the world was at my fingertips. I was a Yale grad biding my time in the White House's Chief Economic Adviser's office until I would settle on one of many offers for which I could use my eccentric study of and passion for Arabic and Islam. The economy was booming and so was I.

The TV buzzed away in the corner. Another plane into another building? "Hardly," I replied, "it's just double reporting about a terrible accident." Then a staffer ran down the hall to me.

"They hit the pentagon." OK, we were under full attack. China, Russia? Didn't matter. I knew my office, the White House, was the next intended target. Turns out I was right.

I fled. My parked car was blocked in, so I ran three miles home. My house in DC was the residence of the former Japanese ambassador and had a well-fortified basement supposedly capable of withstanding Cold War attacks.

That would be the last time I would run away.

I felt ashamed, but mainly I was angry.

Fortunately, I spent the summer before my senior year at Yale at the Marine Corps Officer Candidate School. Graduation did not mean I had to sign up. In fact, all the cleaning of rifles and drilling completely turned me off to the military. I arrogantly had no intention to sit on some base in southern California and "waste" my 20s away.

But now I was thankful for that summer training. I commissioned across the river from ground zero in a drive-by swearing-in in my old jeans. I wanted blood.

Four years later, staring into that hole in the Ramadi dirt, I realized I was doing exactly what Usama bin Ladin wanted me to do. I, along with much of the country, was playing out a seismic war that would give this heretic more glory and fame than he deserved and would help radicalize people that might otherwise have wanted nothing to do with al-Qa`ida, terrorism, or any kind of violence.[1]

Iraq reminded me of my Atari video game consul in the early 1980s. I had a broken asteroids game. No enemy spaceships were visible. And my laser was impotent, even though there was no visible adversary at which to aim in the first place. All I could do was fly around the stars searching for nothing. When I stopped moving, the nearest star would expand until it just blew up, rendering me dead and the game lost. My very presence would cause this alien universe to turn against me. Instead of returning the defect of a game for

---

[1] I must note that I feel the mission in Iraq essential and the protection of Iraq's innocents a great and noble priority. I am proud to have served and only regret that I did not do more. I am also honored to have supported heroes whom I will never forget.

an easy refund, I held on to it, mesmerized with its insanity. This is how I felt in Iraq.

So I left the Marines to attempt to construct strategies to actually defeat al-Qa`ida. However, with regard to Iraq, I knew that as long as our corporals and sergeants were in the field, we would inevitably push the terrorists out of Iraq. Inevitably, I believe, Marines and Soldiers succeeded with this impossible mission through brilliance and heroism that had nothing to do with the Generals, planners, consultants, and "new" publications of old theories on counterinsurgency. The heroes I did my best to support simply did not know how to fail. Of course, there is a mountain of academic investigatory research that must be conducted over the next decades to figure out what has actually happened in Iraq. In my personal experience, I saw dedicated corporals and sergeants succeed despite planners' and officers' ideas of un-useful conventional warfare.

But I wanted true and complete victory over al-Qa`ida writ large.

This fire drove me to walk brazenly into the office of the most experienced intelligence officer in the world to become his briefer and assistant. The madman (a.k.a. Charlie Allen, a.k.a. the "pile driver") accepted. I spent the next years studying under him at Homeland Security, taking graduate classes in Islam and Arabic literature, publishing a book on countering radicalization, advising the Department of Defense, and starting a non-profit with one goal: end al-Qa`ida.

But a kinetic mindset[2], even in the new administration it seems, is too entrenched to allow for more long-term strategies that abandon the simple killing of insurgents for an actual plan to defeat al-Qa`ida. Despite a renaissance of the millennia-old methods of counterinsurgency (victory measured in civilians protected instead of enemies killed—not new despite a surge in literature on the subject[3]), the government is still bent on killing

---

[2] "Kinetic", in this book, refers to a military term describing traditional police and military violent operations.

[3] The United States alone has developed a wealth of counter-insurgencyand insurgency lessons and literature from military campaigns including the "Indian Wars" campaigns east and west of the Mississippi from 1775–1890; Revolutionary War guerilla operations from 1775–1783; skirmishes behind battle lines during the Civil War from 1861–1865; the Philippine insurrection from 1899–1902; counterinsurgency in Haiti from 1915–1934; support for anti-Germany insurrections in Europe and anti-Japan insurrections in Asia during the Second World War from 1939–1945; support for counterinsurgencies in Vietnam, Laos, and Cambodia from 1959–1975; support for the mujahidin against the Soviets in Afghanistan from 1979–1988; counterinsurgencyin Beirut in 1983; counterinsurgencyin Iraq from 2003– present and Afghanistan from 2001– present; and other support for insurgencies and counterinsurgencies in the 20th and 21st century in Southeast Asia, Southwest Asia, sub-Saharan Africa, and South America. The most prominent recent literature, which can be applied to local insurgencies and transnational insurrections alike, include the "U.S. Army Field Manual Number 3-24 / Marine Corps Warfighting Publication Number 3-33/5" (2006), Joint Special Operations University's "Counter Insurgency Operations" (1962, by Lieutenant General William P. Yarborough),

terrorists with no concerted plan for strategic victory. I've published a book, briefed members of
Congress, and spoken to undersecretaries, but my
voice for victory is drowned by voices asking only
for military/police action...so far.

The U.S. government readjusted satellites
and used billions of dollars of intelligence to kill
al-Qa'ida's number three time and again since
2001. But when an event takes place that could
quite literally change the course of history and
ignite revolts against al-Qa'ida, or at the very least
drain violent extremism of support and recruits,
nothing is done. There is no violence of action.

Three moments out of the hundreds come
most prominently to mind because it would have
been so easy with a few hundred-thousand dollars
to strategically injure or even defeat al-Qa'ida
growth. In 2005, extremists strapped a suicide
vest to an Iraqi boy with Down Syndrome. The
Iraqi boy tried to get help from soldiers before the
insurgents ignited him. In 2007, one of al-Qa'ida's
most influential ideologues did a one-eighty and
wrote a book condemning violent extremism. In
2010, local Pakistani news picked up a story of al-
Qa'ida and Taliban members embroiled in a ring
of videotaped rapings of pre-adolescents. In each
case, had the story been translated, amplified,

"U.S. Special Operations Command Strategy 2010" (1 November 2009), and David Galula's "Counterinsurgency Warfare:
Theory and Practice" (1964).

and marketed factually to the world, without spin or exaggeration, by a credentialed source (just as al-Qaʿida does with its messages) other than the distrusted U.S. government, al-Qaʿida's growth would have suffered for years to come. Bottom line: amplifying such stories is worth more than a fleet of B-2 bombers. This book will explain why.

While military public affairs units in warzones still rattle off the number of insurgents killed following operations out of one side of their mouth and re-explain that protecting civilians is the main goal out of the other side, al-Qaʿida and its sister and affiliate organizations grow more deadly. Sometimes they move across borders, just as some insurgents from Iraq and Saudi Arabia have moved into Yemen (and even Somalia), and those in Afghanistan have receded into the countryside or into Pakistan during NATO surges.

Bullets, however, clearly do not kill al-Qaʿida. To the contrary, bullets often strengthen al-Qaʿida, and any action against them legitimates them as a "serious" and seemingly equitable threat to the United States in the eyes of some Muslim communities.

U.S. Department of Treasury Undersecretary for Terrorism and Financial Intelligence Stuart A. Levey wrote a 6 June 2010 Washington Post editorial, in which he states that an al-Qaʿida leader death was a "big blow for al-Qaeda." His analysis is baseless.

He writes:

> *Last month, al-Qaeda was dealt a major blow. In losing Mustafa Abu al-Yazid— also known as Sheik Saeed al-Masri—the*

> *terrorist organization was deprived of one of its founding members and also its third-highest ranking official.*

To think that Yazid, who helped build al-Qa`ida, would not have built in redundancy and trained numerous apprentices with similar leadership acumen, deep-seated personal contacts, and ability to liaison with extremists the world over is fallacy. Al-Qa`ida leaders know they will die. And they plan accordingly.

In Undersecretary Levey's op-ed, he claims that more must be done before the next generation of "Yazids" take over. But to think that the new generation of "Yazids" had not already taken over the moment of Yazid's demise is fallacy. His death is a martyrdom that will further inspire his already prepared trainees and tens of thousands of violent extremists and supporters to come—not to mention that the news reports over the drone attack that killed him will also inspire thousands to support al-Qa`ida, if not actively then passively, by turning a blind eye and not speaking out against al-Qa`ida's terrorism.

Killing leaders may make headlines and bring undersecretaries satisfaction, but al-Qa`ida is no weaker than the day before Yazid's death.

This book will propose a permanent and strategic strategy to defeat al-Qa`ida.

This book is a policy recommendation. My intended audiences are government policy makers, commanders, operators, and analysts worldwide, as well as nonprofit and religious leaders. I also hope that this book inspires every reader to learn more about Islam and methods to counter radicalization.

The policy's goal is al-Qa`ida's defeat.

The proposition is based on exploiting al-Qa`ida's key vulnerability, which I have witnessed in 11 years of field and analytic experience in the counterterrorism and Near East disciplines.

As my mentor in the Marine Corps taught me, if you see the enemy bleed, exploit this success, just as when a boxer's opponent covers his hurt left ribs the boxer will continue driving blows into his opponent's left ribs again and again until victory. In short, if you find an enemy's vulnerability, which will lead to destruction of his key strength, invest everything you have against that area.

When young German infantry officer Erwin Rommel grew sick of leading his platoon into walls of allied machine gun fire in World War I, he developed a strategy to find and exploit enemy vulnerability. Instead of throwing his men across open fields of fire, he would send out scout units judiciously to test enemy capabilities in numerous regions. When young Rommel found an enemy weakness, such as a quarter-mile stretch of the

enemy line where a guard post was not being par-
ticularly attentive with unreinforced positions, he
would gather all possible force and drive straight
through that vulnerable area. He would place engineers, heavy guns, and explosives teams under
his junior command to storm the vulnerability because he refused to allow the enemy a chance at
survival. Once he stormed past the vulnerable
area of the allied lines, he turned his firepower on
the enemy's unprotected flanks, killing or capturing all defenseless and surprised enemy units in
sight. His strategy has informed World War II
German tactics and U.S. infantry tactics to this
day.

Infantry squads as well as an entire nation
at war can employ Rommel's tactic. In short, exploit an enemy's critical vulnerability to destroy its
center of gravity.

An enemy's center of gravity and critical
vulnerability are defined in 1997's Marine Corps
Document Publication 1 "Warfighting," which
states:

> *Center of gravity and critical vulnerability
> are complementary concepts. The former
> looks at the problem of how to attack the en-
> emy system from the perspective of seeking
> a source of strength, the latter from the per-
> spective of seeking weakness. A critical
> vulnerability is a pathway to attacking a
> center of gravity. Both have the same under-
> lying purpose: to target our actions in such a
> way as to have the greatest effect on the en-
> emy.*

Like Rommel, the United States in its fight against al-Qa'ida must throw all it has at the enemy's vulnerability. It must stop reinforcing failure and viciously exploit success. The United States is fortunate because al-Qa'ida has clearly shown its weakness. Al-Qa'ida has bled.

This weakness is al-Qa'ida's violent ideology, most prominently displayed with its wanton *tatarrus*. Tatarrus, Arabic for human shields, refers, in violent extremist circles, to the gratuitous murder of innocents. Wanton tatarrus reveals al-Qa'ida's inhumanity, impiety, lack of vision, failed and ignorant leadership, and inevitable failure (more on this later). When al-Qa'ida, or groups that abide by al-Qa'ida's violent ideology, have focused sustained attacks in one area, the people have tended to revolt. Or, at the very least, people become so disgusted that they gladly allow others, such as government security forces, into their neighborhoods to conduct a counter-revolution to kill the local strands of violent extremists. In 2006, this type of counter-revolution happened in Iraq's al-Anbar province, like in Algeria and Egypt in the 1990s. Even though al-Qa'ida grows (and the group is growing as you read these words), al-Qa'ida still has a limited reach, not yet enough to conduct attacks everywhere and enrage local populations the world over.

My proposal is to inspire social movements to revolt against al-Qa'ida before al-Qa'ida grows further—to incite yet-untouched communities to hate al-Qa'ida before its influence impinges on the community. The proposal in this book is to inspire communities to action before the bloodbaths ensue in their backyards.

How do we know that violent ideology is al-Qa`ida's weakness, besides the examples of Iraq, Algeria, and Egypt? (Extremists did themselves in in Iraq, Algeria, and Egypt by maddening the population to the point at which violent extremism could eventually find no support, no safe haven, and no more recruits.) Because since 2001, Al-Qa`ida has written over a thousand pages defending its unwarranted murder of innocents—openly revealing al-Qa`ida's unprecedented feeling of vulnerability. Al-Qa`ida redirected time and money that could have been used to further its cause, to defensively attempt to cover its key weakness.

When al-Qa`ida's greatest ideologue shifted sides in 2007 and criticized al-Qa`ida's wanton tatarrus and impiety, al-Qa`ida chief deputies put aside their operational responsibilities to write essays and books and conduct interviews and speeches to defend against the accusations. Al-Qa`ida showed its fear over this vulnerability. It bled.

But the United States was not there to twist the knife, to market the counter-al-Qa`ida statements anonymously or through third, unattributable parties in enough languages and media platforms to reach a global audience. The United States and Western counterparts failed to capitalize on the recantation that could have helped serve to inspire communities to repel al-Qa`ida or at least to create environments inhospitable to future al-Qa`ida influence.

This critical vulnerability is so destructive to al-Qa`ida that its exploitation will lead to destruction of its center of gravity: support from a portion of society. I am not referring to wide support in the Muslim world. Al-Qa`ida clearly does not enjoy wide support according to multiple polls conducted over the past decade. Instead, I am referring to small pools of future recruits and all-too-common public non-engagement or indifference which allows al-Qa`ida militants to find safe havens. Army Lieutenant General William Yarborough explained it well in his 1962 "Counter Insurgency Operations," although he was referring to communism-driven transnational insurrections.

> *The basic elements of success of the 'People's War' have rested in the active support of a minority of the target population and the tacit support or neutrality of the balance of the people, due largely to apathy, disgust or open hostility toward the regime in power.*

Despite the obvious critical vulnerability and center of gravity, the United States continues to play right into al-Qa`ida's invulnerable strengths.

Each troop increase in Iraq and Afghanistan creates more sympathy for al-Qa`ida and appears to confirm al-Qa`ida's simple narrative that Islam is somehow under attack.

Each leader killed offers al-Qa`ida greater legitimacy with the appearance of being an equitable U.S. foe. All al-Qa`ida cells are built regeneratively to withstand leadership deaths. Its leaders are easily replaceable.

Each military attack against violent extremists merely drives them to ground or forces them to move, failing to significantly hurt enemy operations in the short run. A New York Times reporter, in Taliban captivity 2008–2009, expressed this phenomenon vividly:

> *We arrived in Pakistan's tribal areas, an isolated belt of Taliban-controlled territory. We were now in "the Islamic emirate" — the fundamentalist state that existed in Afghanistan before the 2001 American-led invasion. The loss of thousands of Afghani, Pakistani, and American lives and billions in American aid had merely moved it a few miles east, not eliminated it.[i]*

Each money network shut down reveals to the world al-Qa`ida's "surprising" resilience. Al-Qa`ida is built to run penniless. Even if they want money, they do not need it. Since 2001, every major terrorist attack has relied on shoestring funding such as fireworks or box cutters. And the most violent extremists have been wealthy—happy to use their own money. Al-Qa`ida are inspirers, not funders.

Each website knocked out of service uncovers the robustness and the regenerative nature of al-Qa`ida's worldwide online marketing network because their websites will resurrect, sometimes in minutes.

I will use the definitions of Dr. Joe Strange, U.S. Marine Corps War College, to conduct a military analysis of al-Qa`ida's critical vulnerability and center of gravity:

> <u>*Centers of Gravity*</u> *- physical or moral enti-*

ties that are the primary components of physical or moral strength, power, and resistance. They don't just contribute to strength; they ARE the strength.

<u>*Critical Capabilities*</u> *- every center of gravity has some primary ability (or abilities) that makes it a center of gravity in the context of a given scenario, situation, or mission...*

<u>*Critical Requirements*</u> *- conditions, resources, and means that are essential for a center of gravity to achieve its critical capability.*

<u>*Critical Vulnerabilities*</u> *- those critical requirements, or components thereof, that are deficient or vulnerable to neutralization or defeat in a way that will contribute to a center of gravity failing to achieve its critical capability.*

This analysis applied to al-Qa`ida:

Center of Gravity

Popular Support - The active advocates of transnational insurrections constitute a small but capable and active segment of the population. This includes the minority of armed militants and terrorists as well as a small portion of supporters who help to legitimize and galvanize the violent extremists.

Although distrust of government due to disillu-
sionment with social and economic conditions is
prevalent in many nations, populations normally
do not have a self-initiatcd inclination to conduct
violent attacks—killing women and children—as a
means to revolt. The public generally desires to be
left to earn money and conduct normal familial,
tribal, and community affairs. Most are apathetic
to the goals of violent extremists and counterterrorism government forces alike.

Critical Capabilities

Defensive Narrative - "Islam is under attack." The
very presence of U.S. forces, no matter to what
end, plays into this narrative and substantiates
al-Qa`ida and affiliates' claims. By example, U.S.
forces provided Tsunami aid in Southeast Asia,
protected Muslims in Bosnia and Kosovo, and
have attempted to stabilize Iraq and Afghanistan.
Despite U.S. assistance, the very existence of U.S.
and allied forces in Muslim-majority countries
plays into al-Qa`ida's narrative and helps drive
support and recruitment. Al-Qa`ida affiliates
worldwide use "Islam is under attack" as an ex-
cuse to fight government forces and Western
interests, shore up support, and earn recruits.
Each regional violent extremist group claims its
region is a central front in the greater war.

Online Marketing - The Internet is a safe haven
from which al-Qa`ida can brand its name and in-
spire lone wolves, those typically educated and
driven by numerous and complex psychological,
social, and personal motivations. Al-Qa`ida's ro-

bust, unchallenged, flexible, and regenerative web network also helps to inspire franchises and sister organizations.

Public Intimidation - While al-Qa`ida disseminates a message of "protecting Islam" through its media, its militant groups and sister organizations employ assassination, intimidation, kidnapping, and punishments to subjugate apathetic or opposed communities in warzones. Examples include the Taliban in Afghanistan, al-Qa`ida in Iraq, and al-Shabaab in southern Somalia. Since the narrative of "Islam is under attack" can only inspire a minority of Muslims, local bullying and killing are necessary for al-Qa`ida and affiliates to operate openly in any given area.

Regenerative Leadership - Central and cell leadership is structured to withstand leadership deaths or capture with as little disruption to militant operations as possible. Although some leadership deaths may cause temporary disturbance, leadership incapacitation will never translate into strategic victory.

Patience - Al-Qa`ida has instilled in its followers the belief that victory[4] will take generations. So when governments step up police and military operations, militants in every theater often go to

---

[4] Victory is a transnational caliphate that abides by al-Qa`ida's interpretation and implementation of religious law. Often individual militants and cells do not think this far out and so adopt the more modest aim of simply killing and dying for what they perceive as religious duty.

ground, temporarily cease activities, and hide. Extremists often simply stop operating until governments lessen efforts, when terrorists can begin planning and recruiting again. Time is on al-Qa`ida's side. An informal saying among some Marines is "we have all the watches, al-Qa`ida has all the time."

Intermarriage - When al-Qa`ida moves to a new area—whether it be Sudan, Afghanistan, Pakistan, or Yemen—its militants quickly endear themselves to locals by marrying into local communities. Through these marriages, al-Qa`ida becomes part of the fabric of that society. Familial relationships offer violent extremists safe haven and bind the locals to the side of al-Qa`ida. When the Yemeni army traveled to arrest al-Qa`ida militants in the Marib province in 2009, soldiers found themselves fighting an entire village ready to fight and die for its new al-Qa`ida kin.

Delivering on Promises - Al-Qa`ida often does what it says. Al-Qa`ida in the Arabian Peninsula promised to attack the West. Counterterrorism analysts dismissed al-Qa`ida's threats as empty illusions of grandeur. I know because I was one of these government analysts who assessed that al-Qa`ida in the Arabian Peninsula would not have the capability, cause, or initiative to attack the West on western soil. Surprisingly, al-Qa`ida delivered on its promise. On 25 December 2009, al-Qa`ida sent 23-year old Nigerian Umar Farouk (wearing PETN explosives concealed in his underwear), to blow up Northwest/Delta Flight 253 in-bound to Detroit. Although unsuccessful, the attempt was nonetheless an act of terrorism and showed al-Qa`ida's reach from the Arabian Peninsula. Likewise, the Taliban warned the United States that it would conduct an attack on U.S. soil. I witnessed analysts in the U.S. security community dismissing such claims as empty bravado. Once again analysts were wrong. The Taliban was found to be behind Faisal Shahzad's attempt to detonate a vehicle-borne improvised explosive device in the heart of New York City. Such connection between words and actions gives al-Qa`ida, its affiliates, and sister organizations credence among violent extremist sympathizers and makes everything these groups say of utmost importance to governments.

Critical Requirements

Fledgling and/or Corrupt Government - Al-Qa`ida's ability to activate and exploit a population lies in basic unresolved challenges within the country. This allows al-Qa`ida and similar militant organizations safe haven:

> *The military contributes but cannot win the conflict without extensive changes and reforms to eliminate the causes of dissension and revolt.*

> *Unless the government achieves an ascendancy of ideology and aims over those offered by the guerillas/terrorists and convinces the people of their intent to implement extensive changes and reform the forces of revolutionary war will eventually win.*[ii]

It must be noted that even without safe haven, al-Qa`ida has been able to execute mass casualty attacks in population centers. This critical requirement only applies to some areas of al-Qa`ida presence and influence, such as southern Somalia, eastern Yemen, and western Pakistan.

Money - Although important for arms purchase and smuggling, human smuggling, pay-offs to tribal and local political leaders, and recruitment of those looking for salary and day-to-day needs, most large-scale al-Qa`ida terrorist attacks require minimal funding. A small amount of PETN explosive, gasoline tanks, or box cutters are all relatively inexpensive. "...A little imagination and planning and a limited budget can turn almost anything into a deadly, effective, and convenient weapon," stated an al-Qa`ida spokesman in March 2010 in English.

"Following the money trail" as thousands of government specialists do to track down terrorists may lead to finding terrorist cells and stopping deadly attacks. But these efforts will never undermine al-Qa`ida. The deadliest terrorists have been wealthy and perfectly capable of operating with cheap supplies without the need for outside funds—from the 9/11 hijackers to the 7/7 London bombers to the failed 2010 Times Square bomber. Even the most impoverished non-ideologically-driven insurgents in Iraq operated with wire stolen from telephone lines, rocket ammunition lying around from Saddam's years, and equipment from trash dumps such as washing machine timers. Al-Qa`ida may want money but certainly does not need it to operate.

U.S. and Allied Presence - The presence of conventional forces often causes alliances of convenience between politically motivated anti-government/anti-"invader" forces and ideologically driven transnational violent insurrectionists. Such presence offers al-Qa`ida recruits, legitimacy, and a materialization of its narrative.

Critical Vulnerability

Violent Ideology – Public backlash could create an impermissible environment for extremists as al-Qa`ida wantonly kills innocents to include mostly Muslims who are non-combatant women, children, elderly, and handicapped. Terror campaigns in Algeria and Egypt in the 1990s and in Western Iraq from 2003–2007 may, in large part, have galvanized populations to act against extremist influences. Massacres of civilians were seen as impious, inhumane, and viscerally repulsive. Not only do such attacks undermine al-Qa`ida's claimed religious legitimacy, since killing non-combatants is clearly prohibited in accepted Hadith and the Quran, but families and concerned citizens fear for their own lives. A media campaign must accurately and emotively expose al-Qa`ida's violent ideology to exploit this vulnerability before al-Qa`ida can reach more territories, more recruits, and further support.

Most Likely Course of Action

Al-Qa`ida will likely continue to inspire some militants willing to kill and die in areas of instability like southern Somalia, the national border regions of North Africa and the Sahel, Yemen, Afghanistan, Pakistan, Chechnya, and pockets of Southeast Asia. Al-Qa`ida, via its worldwide robust and regenerative online marketing and communications network, will also likely continue to irregularly inspire deadly lone wolves such as Nidal Hassan (November 2009 Fort Hood shooter) and Umar Farouk (December 2009 failed airliner bomber).

Most Dangerous Course of Action

Mass casualty attacks are the most dangerous enemy course of action. Most dangerous would be if an al-Qa`ida cell or militant steals and detonates a portable weapon of mass destruction in a dense urban population. Nasser al-Bahri, Usama bin Ladin's former bodyguard, states in his 2010 book *Dans l'ombre de Ben Ladin*, that al-Qa`ida leadership is bent on securing a nuclear device. As bin Ladin reportedly said, "I am prepared to give my entire fortune to have a nuclear weapon in order to arrive at an equilibrium with the Americans."

Contrary to common perception, permanently taking over a region is not a most dangerous course of action. Al-Qa`ida and sister groups have shown little skill for governing or defending against conventional forces as shown in Afghanistan in October 2001 and Fallujah, Iraq in November 2004.

Before I begin my book, I should make a few cautionary comments regarding the strategy to exploit al-Qa`ida's violent ideology.

This policy recommendation must be taken into a holistic whole-of-government and partner nation approach. Although it is the most important strategy the United States can execute to permanently and strategically defeat al-Qa`ida, there are other factors to consider.

For example, the United States must still defend itself against terrorist attacks. Breaking up, arresting, and killing those plotting against the homeland and U.S. interests and persons abroad is still necessary. And the U.S. police and military get better at this every day. It is unfortunate that necessary security considerations stop the literally thousands of successes from being reported.

As we do continue to defend ourselves, we must do so with the best personnel because any organization is only as good as its employees or troops. Most important, in my experience, more linguistic and cultural expertise is necessary to properly define, identify, and neutralize threats. If you think that this is common sense in the government, think again. Before I left the Department of Homeland Security's headquarters intelligence section in 2009, which comprised hundreds of officers, I was the only person who read Arabic.[5]

---

[5] It may also be noted that the Department of Homeland Security denied repeated formal requests for supscriptions to

It is important to emphasize that experts must have a depth of knowledge. Experts are not graduates of the Defense Language Institute's one-year intensive Arabic program. I have struggled with Arabic for 12 years, and there are still worlds for me to learn. As my Yale language professor said to me, "Arabic is for life." Likewise, officers cannot be considered experts just because they graduated from a two-year masters program in Arab studies or one of the other dozens of security/foreign service policy masters programs.

I sat in senior meetings where undersecretaries disparaged security officers for being too strict in withholding security clearances from first- and second-generation immigrant applicants from regions of interest. But as a senior intelligence officer who conducted dozens of candidate interviews, I can attest that it is not the failure of security departments. It is leadership failure for not changing recruitment strategies, which leave true experts in the dust in favor of quasi-policy hacks whose dearth of regional knowledge is surpassed only by lack of imagination and drive. I would prefer a soldier who has completed four tours in Afghanistan and speaks conversational Dari or a Lebanese-American who grew up understanding five Arabic dialects (and the limits of her own biases as well) over a 24-year-old masters graduate whose credentials include a semester

---

mainstream daily Arabic newspapers. I needed a pulse on what Arabic-speaking communities were reading to function in my job. So, I would purchase them myself or travel to libraries to keep up on the latest perspectives and news of the Arab world.

abroad and a college course on the Taliban. If the security offices, who in my opinion show the utmost professionalism and dedication to their mission to protect our nation's most vital information, deny an expert applicant, then it should be within leadership's purview to create offices and billets to employ these persons to work with unclassified information. Unclassified information comprises the vast majority of valuable intelligence on terrorism.

Another consideration before I describe the book's proposal is employing locals to fight extremists in hotspots. As we conduct counterterrorism operations abroad, we must employ the locals under local constructs at all times. In Iraq and Afghanistan, this means tribes. There is a reason tribes have persisted through millennia of imperial rule and anti-tribal policies in areas known today as Iraq and Afghanistan, despite their being seen consistently as a threat to central rule. Tribes are strong. In fact, they are stronger than brutal dictatorships—Saddam Hussein in Iraq, and the Soviets and Taliban in Afghanistan.

I have endured dozens of policy and analyst meetings where sociologists argue over the current strength of tribes and whether their stature is presently waning or growing. But their very existence reveals their persistent strength. If Genghis Khan and Alexander the Great failed to check tribal power in Iraq and Afghanistan, the U.S. president and democratic programs will also be unsuccessful.

A policy of supporting tribes has reaped rewards in recent history. In 2006, U.S. forces in

western Iraq began to pay off tribes to defeat
hardened al-Qa`ida elements in tribal backyards.
From a kinetic perspective, these tribes fared far
better than U.S. troops because the locals knew
the human and geographic terrain far better than
outsiders. Likewise in 2010, U.S. forces began to
pay off tribal leaders to defeat Taliban cells. Dozens of Afghans were armed and trained as
neighborhood watches. In these tribal areas, mar-
kets and schools began to thrive. Improvised
explosive devices ceased, and Taliban attacks
came to a standstill.[iii]

Many in NATO fear the long-term consequences of strengthening locals, such as the
unintended creation of future warlords.[iv] However,
this criticism is largely unfounded. A counterinsurgency strategy must protect locals by any
means, and as quickly as possible. But we should
arm locals in concert with strong liaison with local, provincial, and federal police, much as
neighborhood watches in Washington, DC sometimes work well with both the Metropolitan Police
Department and the FBI.

These tribal support programs may not be
democratic by Western standards, but they work.
There is no genius to this strategy. It is just the
natural operational materialization of acknow-
ledgement of tribal dominance. Colonel T.E.
Lawrence did not ignite an ideological tribal uprising to rout the Ottomans from the Arabian
Peninsula in the First World War. Instead, Lawrence literally paid tribes to conduct primitive
tried-and-true hit-and-run raids against supply
lines.

As NATO commanders fear, arming and

funding tribal leaders, no matter how local defense initiatives are intertwined with official local
and federal police forces, will almost certainly
cause some sort of future civil strife and unfore-
seen second and third order effects. Such risks
are often beneficial in the short run to fight a defined enemy, once weighed using predictive
analysis and a keen understanding of the complex
and competing issues involving tribe and clan
leaders.

A Specialized Discipline

Finally, conventional forces should be avoided—if
possible—when al-Qa`ida's transnational insur-
rection materializes as local insurgencies in
ungoverned territories such as eastern Afghanistan, southern Somalia, and national border areas
between nations of North Africa and the Sahel.
Instead Special Operations Forces or any other
troops specially trained to live and fight locally
should be the main effort, for the following reasons.

Counterterrorism, counter-radicalization
(from supporting those actively opposed to violent
extremists, to inoculating unengaged societies
from extremist influence, to dissuading potential
recruits, to killing and capturing militants
through training and employment of indigenous
units), and civil engagement are specialized and
sophisticated disciplines. According to a traditional definition, Special Forces "means something
very specific—support for resistance movements
battling governments hostile to the United
States."[v]

The Special Forces operator (same can be applied to any troops with special training) should remain the main effort in this discipline. He is:

> *an expert in warfighting skills, executing the core activities, and understanding cultures around the world. Operators execute missions across the 3-D Construct of Defense, Diplomacy, and Development. The Operator is an integrating factor at the lowest level of operations, providing synergy to the application of national instruments of power and providing a tangible mechanism to meet national objectives. All efforts to develop, field, support, enable, and employ a force will focus upon empowering the Operator. This Operator is the building block and foundation of teams and units encompassing USSOF specialists including intelligence... logistics... and communications... as well as other essential functions.*
>
> *The 3-D Warrior is that special operator who is regionally grounded, diplomatically astute, expert in the core activities, and whose actions produce tactical through strategic effect within coordinated whole-of-government approach. In the realm of Diplomacy, the 3-D Warrior understands regional and local interests, and builds long-term trust in support of diplomatic efforts. In the realm of Development, the 3-D Warrior integrates assistance activities with broader interagency and international efforts. In the realm of Defense, the 3-D Warrior brings*

unique skill sets addressing both direct and indirect means. Direct means include those capabilities that aggressively counter adversaries. Indirect means include those capabilities for building partner capacity and establishing long-term relationships.[vi]

Modest Footprint

Special forces or other specially trained Marines, Sailors, Airmen, or Soldiers generally operate with the lowest profile possible because, few in numbers, they tend not to live on forts and only operate in dangerous areas impermissible to mainstream media attention. Without a significant presence of conventional forces or camps, the enemy's recruitment main narrative that "Islam is under attack" collapses and non-ideological anti-"invader" insurgents have nothing to fight. In this way, special forces and indigenous populations are essentially isolating only the ideologically driven violent extremists and staunching their future growth in contested areas. If U.S. presidents in the future feel they need military presence in a certain area without the actual military presence, this may be their best option.

Easy Transnational Movement

Special Operations Command or any transnational borderless military command is able to move and surge operators as necessary to defeat transnational insurrection. Just as al-Qa'ida does not operate within the boundaries of geographic areas of operations, the United States and allies must have the complete bureaucratic freedom to move operators from Iraq to Afghanistan to the Philippines, for example, if a mission requires such movement. Al-Qa`ida recruits, trains, and operates from the Philippines to Diaspora communities in the Caribbean. As it stands today, geographic combatant commands are ill-suited to redistribute forces at a moment's notice if necessary.

If we are to fight a transnational insurrection—one with no respect for national boundaries or international law—we must also have a command that can operate seamlessly throughout the world. This command, since we are at war, must even have full authority over (the sanctity of) the local ambassadors and mission chiefs on defeating al-Qa`ida. This suggestion would upset the entire system of the U.S. international relations establishment. But nine years after 9/11, it is about time the United States and its allies operate to win—by taking away border constraints, which al-Qa`ida ignores. To be effective, the transnational command must use and communicate clearly with embassies and staff in-country. After all, in-country personnel are often the local "experts." Nevertheless, at a time of war—if we are truly attempting to defeat al-Qa`ida—we must give primary authority to a command that has a similar disposition to the enemy and a chance at success. The current system is failing.

Operating in Seams

Special Operations Command or other transnational borderless command are also able to operate in the seams between geographic combatant commands, which al-Qa`ida and affiliates thrive on and count on for operational security. For example, in 2005, Iraqi insurgents observed and communicated the geographic boundaries between allied units' areas of operations. They chose to operate and run lines of communication along these seams. Likewise, militants move, recruit, and operate in the areas between U.S. Department of Defense's Pacific Command, European Command, Central Command, and Africa Command. For example, al-Qa`ida in the Arabian Peninsula and al-Shabaab move militants and arms between Africa and Yemen regularly, eastern European terrorists move to Afghanistan, and some Southeast Asian militants move across the India/Pakistan border for training in Afghanistan.

The phenomenon of extremists operating in the geographic seams is the rule, not the exception. Special Operations Command or another transnational borderless command can operate in these seams without bureaucratic drag and without the need to create special cross-geographic taskforces. Sometimes, as with the movement of militants between Somalia and Yemen, hours or even minutes are crucial.

Control of Information Environment

Special forces or other specially trained troops only operate in contested and dangerous areas, which will curtail media coverage and prevent media embeds. Such an effect will ensure operational security for U.S. and allied forces. Furthermore, it will ensure that the true and accurate stories of civil engagement and community support will be told without bias or agenda, and will keep media sources sympathetic to the violent extremists' cause at bay.

Permanent Operators/Analysts

Special forces or other specially trained troops have operators and analysts who can remain in a country in a continual capacity ensuring continuity of relationships with locals and continuity of mission, as needed. Although most forces would rotate in a counterinsurgency environment, a small cell of perennial operators and analysts may be necessary in some areas to sustain long-term missions. Conventional forces typically do not have the option of leaving a permanent cell in place.

Conventional Forces Provide Critical Support and Surge Capacity

With a transnational military command in the lead, conventional forces can and will be brought to bear according to mission demands. For example, law enforcement advisors will be sent to train local police forces and Marines will be used if the enemy ill-advisedly amasses, such as al-Qa`ida in Iraq did in Fallujah between April and November 2004. The Army Corps of Engineers will be called on to conduct needed construction, and Air Force advisors may be tasked to help train pilots of a fledgling indigenous air force. Conventional forces will play vital roles but cannot be the continuous main effort due to their high-profile presence which feeds local insurgency.

I am touching too briefly on enormous and end-lessly contested policy issues in this introduction to underline that my suggested strategy must be taken in concert with a complete national policy. I am not suggesting that we lessen our ability to win conflicts abroad or to defend ourselves. Instead, I am suggesting that the United States maintain its security as it also seeks to strategically defeat al-Qaʿida, understanding that a "checkmate" strategy will eventually remove or reduce the onslaught of al-Qaʿida threats and need to fight al-Qaʿida cell by cell.

Some insightful critics who reviewed my first book, "How You Can Kill Al Qaeda," considered me partial to peaceful approaches since it described a media campaign to discredit al-Qaʿida and inspire revolts against violent extremism, ideas further explored in this book. However, I am not biased toward any type of strategy. I propose the strategy in the earlier and current book because past evidence and current understanding of al-Qaʿida reveal that a campaign to empower Muslims to collapse international insurgency will likely work. If my research and analysis revealed that dropping a judiciously aimed atom bomb would defeat al-Qaʿida, then this is the approach I would suggest. But there is no kinetic answer to permanently defeating al-Qaʿida.

So if you wish to learn an approach against al-Qaʿida that will save trillions of dollars, thousands of lives, and future generations from fighting our war, then please read on and consider the strategy in this book. The lessons in this book can and should be applied to defeating all violent transnational insurrections. While this book focuses only on al-Qa`ida, it is also a blueprint to defeat any actor that operates like al-Qa`ida, religiously driven or not. The theory of this book is applicable to other groups: use al-Qa`ida's critical vulnerability (violent ideology) to deny its center of gravity (support and future recruits).

1. EXECUTIVE SUMMARY

This book will be divided simply into two sections: 1) problem, in which I define al-Qa`ida, its ideology, and its marketing, and 2) proposed solution, in which I describe how to empower Muslim voices to isolate and defeat al-Qa`ida permanently.

Problem

Al-Qa`ida is, at this very moment, a threat to U.S. national security. Al-Qa`ida leadership effectively inspires Muslims to kill U.S. citizens. Through its unchallenged messaging to the Muslim public, al-Qa`ida garners its critical support and future recruits.

There is an abundance of influential counter-al-Qa`ida ideologues. However, these counter-voices lack the reach to inspire general Muslim audiences and thus are unable to undermine al-Qa`ida's violent messages and unable to staunch its growth.

Solution

Amplify and empower counter-al-Qa`ida fighters and theorists to inspire communities and catalyze social movements to isolate al-Qa`ida from Muslim communities worldwide.

Execution

Identify, translate, and amplify persuasive and independent counter-al-Qa`ida voices using the same methods that al-Qa`ida used when it began to build its survivable transnational insurrection.

Is anyone else doing this?

There is currently no effective counter-messaging campaign against al-Qa`ida. This will be the case so long as governments focus on stopping specific attacks at the expense of developing a strategic plan to destroy the root threat: al-Qa`ida's ability to persuade some mainstream Muslims. Police and military operations that arrest and kill al-Qa`ida operators and supporters are measurable and allow government leaders to enjoy only strategically meaningless victories. However, in the face of these measurable successes, al-Qa`ida continues to generate new messages, new operators, and new supporters.

Governments and private groups have attempted limited campaigns to discredit al-Qa`ida, but an effects-based assessment reveals these programs are ineffectual. A simple test is to log online and search for independent and emotive counter-al-Qa`ida statements. As you navigate hundreds of pages of Google hits, you soon realize that no curious would-be extremist or community leader looking for messages to help inoculate youth from al-Qa`ida propaganda can easily find effective inspiration online. If a savvy web user cannot find anything to counter al-Qa`ida, neither can someone who may not even be intending to search for counter-al-Qaʿida narratives in the first place.

It is important to note that this book does not call for any type of propaganda. Simply, it calls for amplifying voices that already exist to accelerate al-Qaʿida's inevitable demise. The book will offer a strategy based on historical data and qualitative assessment of current narratives and trends in Islam.

2. BULLETS DON'T KILL AL-QA`IDA: WHAT THIS BOOK IS NOT

This book does not give directions to stop individual terrorist attacks, something the brave women and men of the U.S. armed forces, allied militaries, and law enforcement do successfully every day. Instead, the book focuses only on strategic and permanent defeat of al-Qa`ida.

The simple elimination of individual extremists in defense of the U.S. homeland and Western interests can be likened to the Greek monster Hydra. For every one head severed, the Hydra would grow two heads in its place. Bullets do not kill al-Qa`ida.

Even if (or when) bin Ladin is offed, his deputies are ready and itching to take over, perhaps with a more violent agenda. For example, Nasser al-Bahri (Usama bin Ladin's former bodyguard) in his book *Dans l'ombre de Ben Ladin,* published in 2010, writes that Usama bin Ladin would use nuclear weapons much more cautiously than his chief deputies if al-Qa`ida had access to such weaponry. And, of course, bin Ladin's death would be seen as a martyrdom and powerful symbol for decades to come.

In fact, although vital to national security, all U.S. defensive and offensive operations have given al-Qa`ida more legitimacy and heightened its ability to recruit. New al-Qa`ida affiliates wear the

U.S. Department of State's terrorist group designation as a badge of honor as al-Shabaab did in its Youtube videos in March 2008. Likewise, public attention paid by the U.S. government has further buttressed al-Qa'ida-supporting star lecturer Anwar al-Awlaki's extremist credentials and influence.

Al-Awlaki's popularity and the audience who watch his online lectures have increased in line with his increased media attention. He has been the subject of public statements on homeland radicalization from Congress and the Executive Office. Government officials' and public admittance that Awlaki is a clear and present danger to the United States and U.S. interests is a badge of honor for Awlaki, who has quoted public testimony of his dangerous nature on his website to bolster his own credentials.

In the 9/11 Commission Report, Awlaki was a named person of interest who was a prayer leader for three of the 9/11 hijackers who were already in the United States preparing their terrorist attack.

In his October 2008 testimony, Department of Homeland Security Chief Intelligence Officer Charles Allen warned, "[Awlaki] targets US Muslims with radical online lectures encouraging terrorist attacks from his new home in Yemen."[6]

---

[6] This is testimony that I drafted for the Undersecretary for the Office of Intelligence and Analysis, Department of Homeland Security—a strategic misstep that was mine and mine alone.

In November 2009, a "For Official Use Only" Department of Homeland intelligence assessment was leaked to the press. The note refers to a 23 December 2008 Awlaki website command for violence and Awlaki's declarations of support for al-Qa`ida affiliate al-Shabaab.[7]

During the November 2009 Senate hearing on the nomination of Caryn Wagner as the new Department of Homeland Security Undersecretary for Intelligence and Analysis, Senator Lieberman (D-CT) stated the following: "For instance, and of real interest, [the Department of Homeland Security Office of Intelligence and Analysis] issued reports at the [For Official Use Only] level to state and local law enforcements in September 2008 and January 2009 on Anwar al-Awlaki, the radical Yemeni-American imam who, according to media reports, was involved in this e-mail correspondence with [Nidal Hassan]."[8]

According to a March 2010 news story, CIA director Leon Panetta spoke about Awlaki's role in inspiring past attacks and Awlaki's goal to "inspire additional attacks on the United States."

U.S. Representative Jane Harman, a member of the House Committee on Homeland Security, stated in Spring 2010 that Awlaki is "probably the person, the terrorist, who would be terrorist number one in terms of threat against us."

President Obama publicly authorized op-

---

[7] I authored this assessment. To date the Department of Homeland Security has not uncovered the source of the leak.
[8] I authored both assessments.

erations to capture or kill Awlaki in April 2010. There could be no greater compliment to Awlaki and no greater method of canonizing a violent extremist enemy of the United States.

With media attention and government warnings, Awlaki's persona may have crossed the proverbial point of no return—when a violent extremist talking head becomes admired enough that his capture or demise would just cause further reverence. The U.S. government has effectively helped to canonize a threat.

In addition, new U.S. government organizations, which al-Qa`ida attacks inspired, are materialized substantiation that al-Qa`ida poses a clear and present danger to the United States. Al-Qa`ida followers and future recruits likely see this government counterterrorism growth as evidence that al-Qa`ida is a viable and successful threat perhaps on level with the former Soviet Union.

Al-Qa`ida terrorism drove the U.S. government to create the Department of Homeland Security, Office of the Director of National Intelligence, and National Counterterrorism Center. Al-Qa`ida terrorism was the impetus for creating state and local intelligence and information field offices in most big cities and for motivated cities, such as New York, to found their own intelligence and anti-terror units. Furthermore, universities around the country have created new Arab, terrorism, and homeland security studies programs in response to al-Qa`ida. If you add in the contractors and support offices built into federal, state, local, and private organizations, the number of personnel runs into the tens of thousands.

Perhaps expansion is necessary to thwart terrorist attacks. However, there is a byproduct: expansion raises the bona fides of just a few men who possess the ability to inspire others to attack.

3. INSPIRING REVOLT

Al-Qa`ida will destroy itself. Just as with past violent extremist movements, al-Qa`ida's indiscriminate killings will cause populations to turn against their aggressors, eventually. It is only a matter of time, as al-Qa`ida continues to grow in its ability to recruit militants and supporters.

I served in Ramadi, Iraq in 2005, when a group of men and women dragged an al-Qa`ida cell out of the city and set the cell's cars on fire. These civilians had had enough of al-Qa`ida's indiscriminate killing of innocents and the very presence of violent militants which forced the United States to send waves of troops to the area. The panicked expulsion reflected a growing public hatred of al-Qa`ida that, in turn, helped the populace to later accept and support the "Anbar Awakening." During the Anbar Awakening, the United States-backed tribes killed militants and helped dissuade would-be terrorists from joining the hardened al-Qa`ida elements in western Iraq.

Likewise, Algeria's Armed Islamic Group wrought so much death between 1992 and 1999—the civil war killed 150,000–200,000 persons—that it isolated itself completely from the population and lost any semblance of popular support. Essentially, the group withered without recruits and without safe havens. Even if the government had not cracked down harshly against militants,

the Armed Islamic Group could not have continued at the time absent its supply of fresh recruits,
support, and safe havens.

Egypt also saw displays of public disgust
over hundreds of innocents killed at the hands of
the Egyptian Islamic Jihad and Gama`a Islamiyya.
The Egyptian Islamic Jihad militants eventually
had so little support that they were forced to flee
to Pakistan and then Sudan.

The U.S. and other governments, along
with concerned citizens, can simply wait until al-
Qa`ida has no sanctuary after it has killed too
many innocents. This may take decades or centuries and cause tens or hundreds of thousands
more lives.

Alternatively, we can close the emotional
space between al-Qa`ida and populations yet un-
affected by al-Qa`ida's influence. In other words,
speed up the inevitable hatred against al-Qa`ida
without the ensuing bloodbaths.

This book chooses the second, more active
and moral strategy.

Defeating al-Qa`ida will first require an ac-
curate analysis of al-Qa`ida's nature as well as its
strengths and weaknesses. Al-Qa`ida is first and
foremost a media organization. It is comprised of
an Egyptian core that is hiding along the Afghani-
stan/Pakistan border and that inspires others to
attack. Its fuel is the simple narrative that Islam is
under attack. Its vehicle is foremost the Internet,
which is its virtual safe haven far more powerful
than any geographic safe haven. In this book, I
will suggest using lessons learned from al-Qa`ida's
media strategy against al-Qa`ida.

Just as al-Qa`ida uses a robust network of

disparate web forums to translate and market its message to inspire recruits and supporters, I will suggest an online (and also offline) strategy to translate and market messages to deny al-Qaʿida recruits and supporters.

Just as al-Qaʿida successfully radicalizes Muslims with its message of "Islam is under attack," the proposed counter-messaging will radicalize Muslims against al-Qaʿida with the accurate message "you are or will soon be under attack from al-Qaʿida."

Practically speaking, this proposed campaign would not normally directly inspire someone to suddenly take up arms against al-Qaʿida just as al-Qaʿida messages normally do not inspire Muslims to independently and suddenly take up arms against the West. Although this does occur, it is not the norm. Instead, charismatic leaders, groups of friends, families, neighborhoods, mosque leaders, or inspired lone wolves, armed with emotive anti-al-Qaʿida messages, may help to inspire inoculation or even active revolt against al-Qaʿida.

Just as al-Qaʿida's messaging catalyzes social movements or individual action over time, counter-al-Qaʿida messaging can be a catalyst for anti-al-Qaʿida campaigns. These campaigns may take on many forms. However, like al-Qaʿida's marketing, anti-al-Qaʿida campaigns can begin on the flexible, anonymous, and ubiquitous worldwide web.

The strategy will be to isolate al-Qaʿida from any Muslim community that might provide it with any type of future support so that al-Qaʿida withers and dies alone and impotent. The logic is that most (but certainly not all) al-Qa`ida hardened violent extremists are beyond rehabilitation. Instead of just trying to de-radicalize the already radicalized, we must dry up future recruits and support. We must drive an irreparable wedge between al-Qa`ida and Muslim communities worldwide that al-Qa`ida depends on for recruits, safe haven, moral support, and legitimacy.

This end state requires engaging all segments of Muslim communities. Included are the few who are already actively opposed to violent extremism, the vast majority who are apathetic and unengaged, those who are currently unengaged but may have a propensity to support or join violent extremism in the future, and those who currently support violent extremists.

The following is a simplistic breakdown of many Muslim communities and the desired effect the strategy in this book works towards:

Those Actively Opposed to Violent Extremism

Solidify the beliefs of those against militants. Provide ideological justification and further inspiration for anti-extremist movements already in action.

Examples of those already against violent extremism are the Pakistani Lashkars—tribal militias who use their own money and weapons to independently defend against or offensively fight Taliban cells encroaching on their territories. On the Afghan side of the border, there are some villagers also fighting the Taliban and al-Qa`ida elements on their own. For example, in June 2010 in Gizab (100 miles from Kandahar), a shopkeeper rallied villagers fed up with the Taliban's presence and intimidation. Dozens of untrained citizens took up arms and pushed the Taliban from their town, which "sits at the apex of a capillary-like infiltration network that connects western Pakistan's lawless tribal regions to key parts of southern Afghanistan." What pushed these regular townsmen to arms? The Taliban, up to that point, had seized trucks, stolen cargo, waged unlawful taxes, tore down schools, took over health clinics for themselves, and kidnapped locals. Eventually the shopkeeper raised over 300 men to execute defensive foot patrols and maintain checkpoints. 14 neighboring towns—inspired by Gizab—have raised similar defense forces. Whether this can be sustained only time will tell— the villagers may need training from the U.S. Special Forces, money from the Afghan government, and moral motivation to sustain a defensive stance against the Taliban in the long run.[vii]

A less violent example is the father of Umar Farouk (the 25 December 2009 failed bomber of an airliner near Detroit). The dad walked into the U.S. Embassy to share his concerns that his son may have joined al-Qaʿida ranks. Unfortunately, the father's warning was not properly heeded—a major U.S. government failure.

A third example is Munich's Darul Quran mosque imam Hesham Shashaa. He personally reaches out to youth to dissuade them from violent extremism. He actively keeps up to date on the latest al-Qaʿida messaging so that he knows what he is up against—he even squirrels away literature that is illegal in Germany so that he remains a step ahead of the terrorist recruiters and supporters.

Although he has lost pupils to terrorist recruiters, he has also claimed successes. For
example, one of his current bodyguards is a martial arts and weapons expert with experience in
the Jordanian military. As recruiters and friends
were coaxing him to become a foreign fighter in
Iraq, Shashaa interceded successfully. He explained to his now bodyguard that religious war
may be permissible sometimes but never the killing of women and children—joining al-Qa`ida can
never be an option.

Mr. Shashaa has stated in interviews that
he believes that "jihad" is part of Islam, "But it
must be the head of state or caliphate who an-
nounces jihad...It can't be someone like bin Laden
or Mullah Omar who declares jihad...What they do
is not jihad." He has said, "If you can show me in
the Koran or Sunnah that I am wrong, I will be the
first one who would take a gun and join them, but
you won't be able to find anything like that."[viii]

With a Palestinian father, he grew up and
studied in Egypt and worked as a journalist. In
short, he has the background, training, and practice to be an excellent communicator—a deadly
weapon against al-Qa`ida's recruitment efforts.

Mr. Shashaa would benefit greatly from an
online competing narrative forum that offers
translations of emotive and accurate counter-
extremist arguments. He needs a toolbox of information and sources to stay steps ahead of al-
Qa`ida. He needs support so that he can continue
his difficult one-on-one work to peal away the appeal of al-Qa`ida's mystique and narrative.

Those actively opposed to al-Qa`ida may be armed anti-extremist militants, concerned citizens willing to alert authorities, or active prayer leader counter-recruiters.

The Apathetic Majority

Catalyze social movements to join those already actively opposed to violent extremism by causing the unengaged majority to react emotionally to violent extremist operations, even if presently they are not directly affected by al-Qa`ida operations.

Inoculate those populations from violent extremist influence, violent extremist propaganda, and violent extremist marketers.

Inspire communities to create environs impermissible to any al-Qa`ida element, sympathizer, or supporter through social movements and societal vigilance against violent extremist influences. The goal is to inspire the vast majority of apathetic Muslims to copy the example of Umar Farouk's father: to live vigilantly and speak out when violent extremism encroaches on one's community. The goal, when possible, is also to inspire some to join the ranks of groups like the anti-Taliban Pakistani Lashkars and active counter-recruiters like Shashaa.

Those Susceptible to Radicalization

Help the indigenous societies and community leaders to dissuade would-be radicals from joining violent extremism. Keep the fence-sitters on the peaceful or even anti-al-Qa`ida side.

This is the traditional arena of the

"counter-radicalization" discipline in government counterterrorism units. The goal is radicalization prevention. The goal is to inspire that young person, who might bc curious about the allure of al-Qa`ida, to feel revulsion over the inhumanity and impiety of al-Qa`ida's bloodlust.

The short-term goal is to nudge those susceptible individuals onto the peaceful side of the ideological fence.

The long-term goal is to inspire them to take a more active role against al-Qa`ida, whether with words or bullets.

Radicalized Militants

Create doubts in some al-Qa`ida affiliates who may not be completely ideologically focused. Such a change for militant affiliates would demand reconciliation with their former violent theology, reconciliation with former foes (the government and prior indigenous competitors like the Lashkars), and acceptance of the looming threat of retaliation from al-Qa`ida.

Force radical militants and their spokesmen to defend their actions and violent ideology, thus bringing more light to their ideological weaknesses, wasting their time (which could otherwise be spent on recruiting, planning, and operating), and making them appear weaker to would-be recruits and supporters.

Rehabilitate[9] hardened radicals in prison

---

[9] For this book I will broadly add disengagement (from violence without forfeiting ideology) to the rubric of rehabilitation. I invite the reader to investigate the wealth of

when possible. There have been dozens of itera-
tions of prison rehabilitation programs from Libya
to Saudi Arabia to Yemen to Kuwait to Malaysia to
Indonesia.[10] No program has allowed ample independent verification of claimed success such as
reports of lower recidivism rates. No program has
allowed independent study on whether those cho-
sen for rehabilitation are pre-selected to be
already personally prepared to disengage from violence. And little study and not enough time has
passed to observe whether governments will thor-
oughly follow up with those released—even
programs that make families responsible for the
newly rehabilitated—to ensure they stay the non-
violent path. In short, the debate as to whether
violent extremists are rehabilitatable will not end
unless studies are allowed to verify claimed government successes.

---

new reports on rehabilitation programs, principles, and methodologies (application of which must be dependent on time,
culture, and location). This discipline goes beyond the scope
of this book, but is essential to understanding and implementing holistic counter-radicalization programs.

[10] In Southeast Asia, some governments offer spiritual rehabilitation, training in nonviolence (using Ghandi and Dr. Martin
Luther King literature), interaction with seasoned religious
scholars, psychological therapy with medication if necessary,
vocational training for efficacy and skills upon release, business liaison for future jobs, familial and tribal integration with
professional counselors present, sports recreation with prison
guards, and training in literature and art as a healthy means
of expression. Although this is promising, more independent
study must be conducted to evaluate prison rehabilitation and
reintegration programs.

Also, when studying prison rehabilitation, one must also study how much governments are separating prison populations judiciously to keep prisons from becoming radicalization caldrons (in Iraq, Egypt, and Yemen, for example, simple criminals are in proximity to radicalizers and often can become terrorists upon release).

Graduates from prison rehabilitation and disengagement programs also integrate into dynamic environments. Changes in foreign policy, proximity to un-rehabilitated hardened radicals, and new terrorist group propaganda may affect recidivism rates. Furthermore, judicial corruption, prison system competence, and overall government buy-in to such prison de-radicalization efforts may affect outcomes.

In summary:

- Solidify beliefs of those already against al-Qa`ida.

- Provide ideological justification for operational counter-extremist movements.

- Mobilize apathetic communities and catalyze social movements.

- Inoculate populations from future violent extremist influence.

- Create environments impermissible to al-Qa`ida and its ideology.

- Dissuade potential militants.

Sow seeds of doubt among some al-Qa`ida affiliates and supporters.

- Force al-Qa`ida onto the ideological defensive.

None of these tactics is inherently peaceful and none calls for understanding or respecting the West, secular governments, or even mainstream Islam. The goal, rather, is to brew a level of disgust strong enough so that communities rebel against al-Qa`ida supporters, members, and influence. The aim is for communities to execute a version of the Spanish Inquisition to verbally or violently rout al-Qa`ida presence of any type and inoculate youth from ever participating in violent extremism in the future. The objective can be restated as "to radicalize Muslims against al-Qa`ida."

When proposed with this objective, analysts frequently offer a counter-hypothesis: when executing a negative campaign (an anti-al-Qa`ida campaign in this case), one must replace a negative concept with an equally impelling positive concept. Applying the hypothesis to al-Qa`ida, one should perhaps replace violent extremism with a movement for democracy, understanding, prosperity, or political participation.

However, communities must determine the next step for themselves, not Western governments. Some communities may resemble the status quo pre-al-Qa`ida, while others may strengthen tribal ties or elect to enter political processes. Propaganda aimed toward swaying the goals of Muslim communities reeks of imperialistic hubris. The arrogance of pushing Western democracy in the Arab world, for example, has often failed and caused unnecessary exacerbation of anti-Western sentiment, likely helping al-Qa`ida to find some sympathizers.

Other analysts underestimate the overall effect of a negative campaign. They claim that a purely negative campaign simply does not work, whether against a violent transnational insurrection or an incumbent in a democratic election.

However, negative campaigns can be effective. Exemplifying the effectiveness of a negative campaign is Al-Qa`ida itself, which was built on the epithet "Islam is under attack." This aphorism is defensive and negative. The proposal in this book appropriates al-Qa`ida's strategy.

4. CONCEPTS EXPLAINED

Before reading further, it is important to understand certain assumptions, definitions, and
concepts. There are many understandings of the
following terms, and each term deserves a wealth
of literature.

The following definitions will serve as a
baseline as I further define al-Qa'ida and a proposed campaign to collapse its transnational
insurrection.

The following are the most important (and
often contentious) to this policy proposal and to
the counter-radicalization discipline as a whole:

<u>Al-Qa'ida core</u> - Regenerative elusive leaders (to
include Usama bin Ladin and Ayman al-Zawahiri)
probably living in western Pakistan who attempt
to inspire individuals and groups to conduct violence in the name of al-Qa'ida.

<u>Al-Qa'ida affiliate</u> - Person or group who explicitly
adheres to al-Qa'ida's core violent ideology.

<u>Al-Qa'ida narrative</u> - Islam is under attack.

<u>Al-Qa'ida ideology</u> - The only way to defend Islam,
which is under attack, is through offensive violence, to include killing innocents in the process.

There are no alternatives to violence to defend Islam.

<u>Al-Qa`ida goal</u> - To create and lead an imagined international state run by al-Qa`ida's rules. Al-Qa`ida has failed to specify how it would exactly interpret or implement its peculiar interpretation of religious law. Al-Qa`ida has failed to explain how this international "caliphate" will be somehow harmonious and homogenous when history's Islamic empires were anything but. Of note is that few militants, according to interviews of failed suicide bombers for example, carry this long-term goal. Instead, interviewees relate only to the more short-term and accessible narrative that Islam is under attack.

<u>Violent extremist/violent radical affiliated with al-Qa`ida</u> - Someone who believes he kills and/or dies in the name of God on behalf or through the inspiration of al-Qa`ida. Violent Extremists are not those who only use words of support for al-Qa`ida or hold anti-U.S. sentiment. This term refers only to those who make the cosmic leap from harmless and sometimes healthy rhetoric to picking up arms to fight and die in the name of al-Qa`ida.

<u>Terrorism</u> – A tactic to create wider societal terror from an action—the psychological result being greater than the damage from the actual attack. Psychological societal resilience can damage the effectiveness of terrorism.

<u>Terrorist</u> - A person who perpetrates acts of violence to spread wider societal fear—who executes tactics of terrorism.

<u>War on Terrorism</u> - A nonsensical phrase that can only be interpreted as a war against a martial tactic. Terrorism is a tactic. The term "war on terrorism" makes as much sense as a "war against the method of frontal armor assaults in warfare."

<u>Muslim community</u> - A neighborhood, town, tribe, or congregation of Muslims, either virtual or real.

<u>Marketing/Messaging</u> – A process or technique to promote, sell, and distribute a product or idea.

<u>Tatarrus</u>[11] - A word used by Al-Qa`ida and al-Qa`ida critics to mean "human shields," often used in justifying the killing of innocents in warfare.

<u>Wanton Tatarrus</u> - A qualitative judgment of gratuitous mass murder of bystanders.

---

[11] Tatarrus holds the Arabic consonants "t," "r," "s" referring to a shield. According to *Al Mawrid* dictionary (M. Ba'albaki, Dr. Rouhi Baalbaki, Dr. Rouhi Baalbaki, Dar El-Ilm Lilmalayin) the verb *tarras* means "to shield or provide with a shield." According to the *Arabic-English Dictionary: The Hans Wehr Dictionary of Modern Written Arabic (*Spoken Language Services, 1993), the noun *turs* (plural *atras* or alternatively *turus*) means "shield."

<u>Jihad</u> - An internal struggle or politically sanctioned martial effort to defend communities and religion.

<u>Jihadist</u> - Someone who conducts jihad. This term will not be used in the context of al-Qa`ida (except in quotations and in the context of discussing laws and philosophy in Islam generally) because jihad is a legitimate and sanctioned phenomenon in Islam. Coupling this term with anything connected to al-Qa`ida would justify al-Qa`ida's violent tactics, impiety, and inhumanity.

<u>Moderate Islam</u> - A nonsensical term that erroneously assumes Islam is inherently extreme or dangerous, thus requiring the adjective "moderate" to temper misperceptions that Islam has an innately extremist nature. Even if Islam were somehow inherently violent, most Muslims are not violent.

<u>Extremist Islam</u> - An inane term that couples a religion to violent extremists who do not display attributes of the religion, perhaps to the point that they forfeit the very religion they profess to defend. The danger of this misnomer is that it justifies violent extremists' actions by considering them part of Islam, which does not resemble al-Qa`ida's violent ideology.

<u>Mainstream Islam</u> - Islam practiced by most Muslims. No two Muslims share the exact same outlooks or beliefs, as with all religions. Islam is furthermore split into factions and separate schools of law. Mainstream Islam refers to the

commonalities among Muslims over the five pillars of religion and the basic premise that wantonly killing innocents is inhumane and impious.

<u>Violent Extremist Insurgents</u> - refers to insurgents who take up arms against those perceived (rightfully or wrongfully) to be foreign invaders or take up arms out of necessity, such as for money and food for survival. They may have no interest in joining the ideologically driven transnational insurrection writ large. Reconciliation may work with these persons to tear them away from al-Qaʿida if they are morally able to reconcile with the entity offering reconciliation and are able to protect themselves from al-Qaʿida retribution. Unfortunately for analysts, this pool often distorts data in terrorism surveys and studies. They raise counts of al-Qaʿida militants and counts of al-Qaʿida and affiliate attacks in Iraq and eastern Afghanistan.

<u>Radicalization</u> - the process or change someone undergoes from being nonviolent to conducting violence (in this book conducting violence in the name of a violent transnational insurrection).

<u>Counter Radicalization</u> - A security discipline that sometimes narrowly describes the mission to prevent radicalization and/or to rehabilitate those who are already radicalized. However, the discipline includes a holistic approach to engage many sections of Muslim communities:

- Strengthen those already repelling radicalization (kinetically, textually, and verbally).

- Inspire the unengaged to repel radicalization (to join the first group in the list).

- Dissuade those susceptible to radicalization from joining the radicalized. (Encourage them instead to become apathetic or to actively repel violent extremism.)

- Rehabilitate those already radicalized. (This is rare, and foreign government rehabilitation programs lack independent verification of claimed successes.)

- Persuade violent radicals to disengage from violence—even if they maintain extremist views.

- Persuade rehabilitated and/or disengaged violent extremists to reintegrate into society.

- Render inoperable or curb the ability of recruiters/inspirers/radicalizers.

5. AL-QA`IDA MARKETING
ITS NARRATIVE

Al-Qa`ida's simple narrative that Muslims are under attack affords al-Qa`ida status as the "opposition" to the current world order. The narrative also helps those angry with the United States and current regimes to more easily empathize with violent extremism. The luxury of opposition allows al-Qa`ida to assume a nonspecific brand name under which normally disparate factions can unite under one umbrella.

Facts and pictures illustrate al-Qa`ida's narrative of Islam under attack from the West. Images of Guantanamo and Abu Ghraib display the United States humiliating Muslims and aid al-Qa`ida with new recruitment pools and public support—even today.

Al-Qa`ida core leadership has referenced Guantanamo's detention facility approximately four or five times per year through 2009. Al-Qa`ida's disparate affiliates have also referenced Guantanamo in over two dozen statements since 2003. For example, the 24 January 2009 announcement of Yemeni and Saudi al-Qa`ida affiliates' merger into "Al-Qa`ida in the Arabian Peninsula" played footage of Guantanamo. These references provide emotionally stirring evidence that Islam is under attack. Pictures of dead Iraqi women and children during the 1990s (post-

Desert Storm) U.S.-led Operation Northern and Southern Watch bombing campaigns in Iraq lent similar images to al-Qa`ida's first recruits.

Al-Qa`ida's message may even have helped to alarm Muslims abroad over U.S. intentions. A majority of Muslims view the United States as a potential threat. According to a 2008 Pew study, majorities in Bangladesh (93 percent), Morocco (92 percent), Indonesia (85 percent), Malaysia (81 percent), Turkey (77 percent), Palestinian Territory (73 percent), Pakistan (73 percent), Jordan (67 percent), Egypt (65 percent), Lebanon (64 percent), and Kuwait (63 percent) were "very" or "somewhat" worried that the United States could become a military threat.[ix] The Muslim world distrusts the U.S. government.

Violence in the name of Islam has even become a fad in some Muslim countries. "Jihadi cool," distrust of the United States, and hatred for U.S. "humiliation" of Muslims have permeated Muslim communities worldwide.[x] Al-Qa`ida has helped to unify some parts of the Muslim world against the United States.

Al-Qa`ida has stayed on message from its inception. From the beginning, al-Qa`ida warned Muslims of the "U.S. threat against Islam." As the U.S. government continues its missions in Southwest Asia and the Middle East, no matter how vital for international security and important for the protection of Muslims, the United States plays out al-Qa`ida's message.

Usama Bin Ladin and his chief deputy, Ayman al-Zawahiri, published their narrative in a 1998 newspaper treatise. They continue to consis-

tently stay on message that "Islam is under attack:"

United States in the Arabian Peninsula:

> *First, for over seven years the United States
> has been occupying the lands of Islam in the
> holiest of places, the Arabian Peninsula,
> plundering its riches, dictating to it rulers,
> humiliating its people, terrorizing its neigh-
> bors, and turning its bases in the Peninsula
> into a spearhead through which to fight the
> neighboring Muslim peoples. If some people
> have in the past argued about the fact of the
> occupation, all the people of the Peninsula
> have now acknowledged it. The best proof of
> this is the Americans' continuing aggression
> against the Iraqi people using the Peninsula
> as a staging post, even though all its rulers
> are against their territories being used to
> that end, but they are helpless.*

United States in Iraq:

> *Second, despite the great devastation in-
> flicted on the Iraqi people by the crusader-
> Zionist alliance, and despite the huge num-
> ber of those killed, which has exceeded one
> million...despite all this, the Americans are
> once again trying to repeat the horrific mas-
> sacres, as though they are not content with
> the protracted blockade imposed after the fe-
> rocious war or the fragmentation and
> devastation. So here they come to annihilate
> what is left of this people and to humiliate*

their Muslim neighbors.

U.S. support for Israel:

> *Third, if the Americans' aims in these wars are religious and economic, the aim is also to serve the Jews' petty state and divert attention from its occupation of Jerusalem and murder of Muslims there. The best proof of this is their eagerness to destroy Iraq, the strongest neighboring Arab state, and their endeavor to fragment all the states of the region such as Iraq, Saudi Arabia, Egypt, and Sudan into paper statelets and through their disunion and weakness to guarantee Israel's survival and the continuation of the brutal crusade occupation of the Peninsula.*

Today, record numbers of U.S. troops in the Middle East, combat operations in Iraq and Afghanistan, and support for Israel continue to provide evidence to support al-Qa`ida's story of Islam under attack from the West. Even well intentioned U.S. operations in Muslim countries fail to assuage Muslim fears. No amount of tsunami aid, earthquake aid, humanitarian missions, Iraqi despots deposed, or Muslims protected (operations in Kuwait, Saudi Arabia, Bosnia, and Kosovo to name a few) appears to temper foreign Muslim anger. These activities actually play directly into the hands of militants who erroneously blame local inequities on the unwanted foreign presence.

By the same token, messages from the U.S. government fall onto deaf or resentful ears. Any U.S. Department of State public diplomacy statement or U.S. military counter-violence state-ment is lost on most Muslims abroad. The United States does not have the credentials in most Mus-lim communities to persuade. Distrust is too deep.

Furthermore, Muslim anti-violence ideo-logues would lose complete credibility, influence, and livelihood through open or rumored collabora-tion with U.S. representatives. Counter messages must therefore come from sources popularly con-sidered independent of governments. Only amplified voices of legitimate independent sources can be effective.

Many persons who have the potential to persuade Muslims are distrustful of the United States. The amplifier/marketer would have to be anonymous groups or persons, independent Mus-lims, or independent publishing companies.

The bottom line is that private citizens can execute the strategy in this book. But because of distrust toward the U.S. and many Western and other secular governments, any government effort would have to be completely anonymous.

6. THE INTERNET &
AL-QA`IDA MARKETING

Al-Qa`ida messages on thousands of websites command Muslims to either kill or support the killing of U.S. citizens to defend Islam against the United States.[xi] Specifically, al-Qa`ida centers its messages on U.S. support for Israel, U.S. troops in Iraq and Afghanistan, and past reported prisoner mistreatment in Guantanamo Bay and Abu Ghraib to rouse anger against the United States and to persuade Muslims that the United States government and U.S. allies repress and humiliate Muslims.

The Internet is the primary media in which al-Qa`ida markets its messages. Al-Qa`ida does not normally use hard literature (books and pamphlets) to garner support. Middle Eastern, Northern African, Southern Asian, and some European governments arrest Muslims who are in possession of extremist or al-Qa`ida-supporting literature. Currently, al-Qa`ida's robust, reinforced, and redundant network of easily accessible online narratives and films in multiple languages and on numerous media platforms is unchallenged.

Empathic media, extremist prayer leaders, extremist Internet web forum hosts and users, and inspirational extremist social leaders (using what is online) amplify al-Qa`ida's message so that the narrative loosely unites violent extremists from the Philippines to the United States.

These disparate elements, from messages originating from the Internet, rally around al-Qa`ida's global narrative that Muslims are under attack and must violently defend themselves. Al-Qa`ida supporters, members, and affiliates use this theme to solicit local recruits and become part of an imagined worldwide operation and ideology. Regional extremist groups often employ unique messages and hooks to recruit and engender support, connecting local grievances to al-Qa`ida's consistent global narrative of Islam under attack.

The Internet offers anonymity, instant worldwide reach, and flexibility. When servers shut down a site, site hosts can resurrect the site almost instantly under another server.

Al-Qa`ida's online flexibility is best illustrated when the extremist organization posts its messages to soccer or body-building blogs (as well as its normal extremist web forums) to ensure survivability of a particular message. In this way, even when private groups or governments shut down terrorist websites, the messages can still be found and later copied and pasted into violent extremist online forums.

While word of mouth is vital, especially in areas lacking Internet access, the Internet has been one of the most common and vital means contributing to an extremist organization's worldwide continuity and growth.

Some analysts suggest that other factors, such as friendships with extremists, peer pressure, and charismatic radical preachers, contribute more to radicalization than Internet messaging. In some cases, such factors may be primary drivers of radicalization. However, online messaging has been the most common vein globally. Studies, government assessments, and al-Qa`ida behavior reveal the centrality of Internet messaging to radicalization:

- In August 2008, the Guardian obtained a British intelligence assessment entitled "Understanding Radicalisation and Violent Extremism in the UK" based on "hundreds" of cases of terrorist recruits, recruiters, and supporters.[xii] One of the study's findings suggests, "People do not generally become radicalized simply through passive browsing of extremist websites, but many such sites create opportunities for the 'virtual' social interaction that drives radicalization in the virtual world. Books, DVDs, pamphlets and music all feature in the experiences of British terrorists but their emotional content—e.g. images of atrocities against Muslims—is often more important than their factual content." The analysis concluded that although interaction with others to include a local charismatic leader was a key driver to radicalization of those studied, online communities were "crucial" and common to cases of radicalization.

- A Homeland Security Policy Institute study of eight major terrorism cases—to include the 2004 Madrid bombers and 2005 London bombers—concludes that online messaging was critical to radicalization.[xiii] Its summary states that:

Cyberspace is now a battlefield for the war of ideas because of its capacity to foster interaction...The internet provides the opportunity for mutual affirmation, which in turn gives rise to a sense of community and belonging in a distinctly egalitarian fashion, a virtual umma that resonates with the Muslim experience. Al Qa`ida is taking advantage of this opportunity and has its own official production arm, which focuses primarily on youth internationally.

- Al-Qa`ida pours money, time, and manpower into its online empire revealing al-Qa`ida's belief that Internet messaging is vital to its continuity and growth. Al-Qa`ida's robust, reinforced, and redundant network of easily accessible online narratives and films in multiple languages and on numerous media platforms employs ever-improving technical expertise, media savvy, and human translation excellence as well as increasing sheer manpower hours.

- Al-Qa`ida affiliates have created professional online media production centers that film, produce, edit, and disseminate films as well as audio and textual messages. The following is a list of media affiliates and the years they were founded:

2001: Al-Sahab, the official al-Qa'ida production company; the following is a chart
that depicts Al-Sahab publications from
2002–2007 (according to counts from the
IntelCenter—IntelCenter.com):

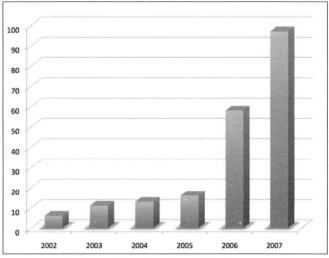

Al-Sahab publications from 2002–2007.

2006: Al-Fajr Media Network—official al-
Qa'ida core online dissemination cell.

2006: Al-Furqan Media Production—official
media cell of the Islamic State of Iraq (al-
Qa'ida affiliate).

2007: Al-Yaqin Media—online media organization   that   supports   al-Qa'ida
worldwide.

2008: Al-Sumud Media—online media group that supports al-Qa`ida worldwide.

2008: Al-Malahim Foundation for Media Production—official online production company of al-Qa`ida in the Arabian Peninsula.

2009: Brigades Establishment for Media—the official media wing of Somalia's al-Shabaab (al-Qa`ida affiliate).

2009: Sada al-Buraq Media—online group established to support al-Qa`ida in the Arabian Peninsula.

2009: Al-Andalus Media Cell—official media section of al-Qa`ida in the Lands of the Islamic Maghrib (al-Qa`ida affiliate).

- According to Saudi Arabia's Al-Sakina program, which attempts to prevent some types of radicalization with Arabic and English online web services (assakina.com and en.assakina.com), English-language Internet sites sympathetic to al-Qa`ida have risen from 30 in 2002 to 200 in 2009. Such sites post English translations of al-Qa`ida or al-Qa`ida affiliate leadership messages as well as messages from bloggers and lecturers supportive of but unaffiliated with al-Qa`ida. The number of extremist sites changes continuously as web addresses change for the sake of security. The rise in English-language sites underlines the overall growth in sheer numbers of al-Qa`ida's many mirror sites.[xiv] English-language sites replay and re-package al-Qa`ida's messages for audiences ranging from Manila to Cairo to Timbuktu to Paris.

• Al-Qa`ida and its supporters have time and again openly advertised for linguists, online marketers, and web technicians to join their extremist cause. These solicitations underline the precedence al-Qa`ida places on improving its online marketing.

• Al-Qa`ida sites have continuously published methods for sites to ease viewership—showing concern for improving online user-friendly features, a customer-based strategy. One example is suggestions to cut down on extremist site banners to ease viewership for those with slow Internet connections. Options are offered to hide banners and bold fonts to offer users more security when viewing extremist sites in public places such as Internet cafes.

• Al-Qa`ida official affiliates and independent media groups have published increasingly sophisticated and attractive online magazines. One example is the English-language online magazine "Defenders of the Truth," which presents a global vision for violent extremism.[xv] The monthly periodical has articles on Somalia, Chechnya,

Uzbekistan, Palestinian territories, Pakistan, Niger, Chad, and Sudan. Essay authors are also reportedly from regions as varied. The magazines are written professionally, praise Usama bin Ladin and Ayman al-Zawahiri often, and cite the Quran and Hadith regularly. The articles range in topic from tactical commentary to philosophical judgments. Each issue can typically be downloaded from at least 15 websites. Because of the easily downloadable format, quality design, at-times almost scholarly-sounding English, and worldwide coverage, this magazine has the potential to sway English readers susceptible to radicalization.

- Other governments have invested time and money in strategies to combat online radicalization under the assumption that Internet messaging is key to the growth of violent extremism. Although the focus of other governments to stop online recruitment fails—by itself—to prove an online threat, the money spent reveals that governments truly buy into the importance of the Internet with regard to radicalization. The confidence in their conclusions corroborates U.S. and UK assessments of the centrality of the Internet to radicalization.

    o Most prominently, the Saudi Government initiated the al-Sakina campaign after it claimed that 70 percent of al-Qa`ida sympathizers were radicalized through Internet messaging. The group has monitored over 400 reportedly "radical" websites and contributed non-violent messages and guidance to these sites directly. Also, Al-Sakina officers hold online discussions directly with supposed extremists, and claim to have de-radicalized 1,170 of 2,631 identified militants.

o   The United Kingdom has the radicalmiddleway.co.uk program among others. Singapore launched the p4peace.com campaign in an attempt to compete with violent extremist online messaging. Note: these websites do not execute the strategy proposed in this book and lack independent evidence of success. Nonetheless, the existence of programs that attempt to curb al-Qa`ida's online presence is circumstantial evidence of the Internet's centrality to al-Qa`ida.

Except in some war-torn and ungoverned territories, the Internet is of the utmost importance to violent extremist groups because hard literature (books and pamphlets) may be dangerous to recruiters and their targets. For example, in Egypt, even possessing copies of deceased-but-still-influential violent extremist ideologue Sayyid Qutb's books is illegal. In short, if al-Qa`ida wants to influence someone, the Internet is the safest and sometimes only method to communicate its message.

Although there is overwhelming evidence that the Internet is the common factor in radicalization, personal interactions and social dynamics in areas like Afghanistan, where only 10 percent of citizens have Internet access, play important roles. But even in these areas, messages that start on the Internet trickle out into night pamphlets (popular with the Taliban) to tribal networks, mosque networks, and word-of-mouth communication.

Further studies are necessary to understand the indirect effects of Internet messages on communities that do not have Internet access. Nonetheless, the fact that groups in areas with little web access still primarily promote their narrative online may be an indicator that Internet messages do affect even audiences without computers.

7. AL-QA`IDA'S MARKETING EFFECTIVENESS

Evidence of al-Qa`ida's marketing success is evident in the growth of official affiliates who forfeit nationalist goals and autonomy, often without clear and present material benefit. This is especially significant in light of the fact that al-Qa`ida members have operated and trained with groups that are not officially part of al-Qa`ida. In other words, affiliation does not appear to be a prerequisite for training and operational support. These groups appear to desire the al-Qa`ida brand for the sake of the brand.

Affiliates include:

Al-Qa`ida in Yemen – Came to prominence with an attack against a U.S. embassy in 2008.

Al-Qa`ida in Saudi Arabia – came to prominence with the Riyadh bombings in 2003.

*Al-Qa`ida in the Arabian Peninsula (AQAP)* – formally merged from Al-Qa`ida in Saudi Arabia and Yemen in a January 2009 statement; located in Yemen and possibly Somalia.

Al-Qa`ida in Iraq (AQIZ) – Abu Mus'ab al-Zarqawi founded in April 2004 and swore allegiance to Usama bin Ladin in October of that year.

*Al-Qa`ida in the Lands of the Islamic Maghrib (AQIM)* – surviving leaders of the Salafist Group for Preaching and Combat aligned with al-Qa`ida in September 2006 and changed its name in January 2007.

Al-Shabaab – militant wing of the Somalia Council of Islamic Courts took over most of southern Somalia in the second half of 2006. Swore allegiance to Usama bin Ladin officially in January 2010.

Taliban – not only do Taliban offer al-Qa`ida protection still today, but also certain elements align with al-Qa`ida's global agenda and ideology.[12]

---

[12] There is anecdotal evidence that the younger generations of Taliban sympathize with al-Qa`ida's agenda. For example, a New York Times reporter—who published his observations from a 7-month kidnapping by the Taliban in Pakistan—observed some Taliban members openly holding worldwide goals. The reporter attests that "[c]ontact with foreign militants in the tribal areas appeared to have deeply affected many young Taliban fighters: They wanted to create a fundamentalist Islamic emirate with Al Qaeda that spanned the Muslim world." Specifically, the Taliban appeared to single out the United States as the Taliban's key enemy: "...Washington's antiterrorism policies had galvanized the Taliban. Commanders fixated on the deaths of Afghan, Iraqi

The reach of al-Qa`ida's marketing is also evident in the number of planned attacks against the U.S. homeland or terrorist acts perpetrated by U.S. citizens. In both cases, al-Qa`ida's narrative moved half a world away to inspire individuals to actually take up arms and plan to kill innocent people. Al-Qa`ida efforts to inspire people far away are encapsulated in a March 2010 video from al-Qa`ida spokesman and U.S. citizen Adam Gadahn, who called on U.S. Muslims to conduct attacks in the U.S. Homeland.

Gadahn stated:[xvi]

> *Brother Nidal [Hassan] is the ideal role model for every repentant Muslim in the armies of the unbelievers and apostate regimes...Nidal Hassan is a pioneer, a trailblazer, and a role model...*

---

and Palestinian civilians in military airstrikes, as well as the American detention of Muslim prisoners who had been held for years without being charged." (New York Times, 18 October 2009, http://www.nytimes.com/2009/10/18/world/asia/18hostage.html)

Circulating on violent extremist websites is imprisoned al-Qa`ida ideologue Abu Musa'ab al-Suri's article "A Drama of Faith and Jihad: the Muhajirin and Ansar" depicting a strong relationship between al-Qa`ida and the Taliban. The article suggests that the Taliban protect al-Qa`ida and that both groups find themselves commonly in a "global confrontation." Although the type and strength of the relationship between al-Qa`ida and the Taliban is contested among analysts, al-Suri's article seems to accurately define the overall protective relationship to this day.

You shouldn't make the mistake of thinking that military bases are the only high-value targets in America and the West. On the contrary, there are countless other strategic places...

...a little imagination and planning and a limited budget can turn almost anything into a deadly, effective, and convenient weapon.

Target mass transportation systems and *[kill]* or *[capture]* people in government, industry, and media.

This statement underscores al-Qa`ida's efforts to call lone wolves and unaffiliated cells to attack the West. The message also demonstrates how al-Qa`ida does not need funding to conduct operations or grow. Al-Qa`ida's core in western Pakistan are not operational militant leaders but primarily inspirers.

Most inspired attacks do not require financial networks or large sums of money. Violent extremist financing, as mentioned earlier in the book, is not a critical vulnerability, and stories that al-Qa`ida is "broke" are inconsequential to appraising al-Qa`ida's current strength and capabilities.

The following cases comprise successful attacks, planned attacks that had a chance of success, and planned attacks that had little chance of success if executed, all inspired by al-Qa`ida marketing. In all cases, al-Qa`ida's narrative was to inspire its operatives into the mindset to kill and/or die according to al-Qa`ida's ideology.

In all cases, al-Qa`ida successfully reached indi-
viduals who might have done damage to the
United States and U.S. interests—al-Qa`ida's ex-
plicit priority target.

2001

U.K. citizen Richard Reid attempts to ignite a shoe
bomb on a flight from Paris to Miami.

2002

Jose Padilla is accused of seeking a radioactive-
laced "dirty bomb" to use in an attack within the
United States.

Six U.S. citizens of Yemeni origin are convicted of
supporting   al-Qa`ida—five   of   six   from
Lackawanna, New York.

Seven individuals (six Americans and a Jordanian
national) from Portland, Oregon are arrested for
attempting to join al-Qa`ida and the Taliban.

2003

Naturalized U.S. citizen Iyman Faris is charged
with plotting to use blowtorches to collapse the
Brooklyn Bridge in New York City.

Eleven men from Alexandria, Virginia ("Virginia
Jihad Network") are charged with conspiracy to
support terrorists.

U.S. citizen Ahmed Omar Abu Ali is arrested in Saudi Arabia for supporting a terrorist organization.

2004

Eight terrorist cell members (led by Dhiren Barot) are accused of plotting to attack U.S. and UK financial institutions.

James Elshafay and Shahawar Matin Siraj are charged with plotting to bomb a subway station near Madison Square Garden in New York City.

Yassin Aref and Mohammed Hossain, mosque leaders from Albany, New York, are charged with plotting to purchase a grenade launcher to assassinate a Pakistani diplomat in New York City.

2005

Father and son Umer Hayat and Hamid Hayat from California are convicted of attending a terrorist training camp in Pakistan.

Kevin James, Levar Haley Washington, Gregory Vernon Patterson, and Hammad Riaz Samana are accused of conspiring to attack National Guard facilities in Los Angeles, LAX, two synagogues, and the Israeli consulate.

Michael Reynolds is charged with planning to blow up gas refineries in Wyoming and New Jersey as well as the Transcontinental Pipeline.

<u>2006</u>

Mohammad Zaki Amawi, Marwan Othman El-Hindi, and Zand Wassim Mazloum from Toledo, Ohio are charged with providing material support to terrorists (making bombs for use in Iraq).

Syed Haris Ahmed and Ehsanul Islam Sadequee from Atlanta, Georgia are accused of conspiring with terrorist organizations (casing and videotaping the Capitol and World Bank for terrorists).

Narseal Batiste, Patrick Abraham, Stanley Grant Phanor, Naudimar Herrera, Burson Augustin, Lyglenson Lemorin, and Rothschild Augustine are charged with plotting to blow up the Sears Tower in Chicago.

Assem Hammoud is charged with plotting to bomb train tunnels in New York City.

U.K. security officials stop a plot (15 charged) to load 10 commercial airliners with liquid explosives to attack targets in the District of Columbia, New York, and California.

<u>2007</u>

Six men are accused of plotting to attack Fort Dix (army base) in New Jersey with assault rifles and grenades.

Four men are charged with plotting to blow up fuel arteries that run through residential neighborhoods at JFK Airport in New York.

2008

A U.S. person is later charged with abetting the Mumbai terrorist attack (which killed 179 people in Mumbai).

2009

A Long Island, New York man pleads guilty to helping al-Qa`ida plot to blow up a train in Penn Station, New York City.

FBI arrests four in a plot to bomb Bronx synagogues and shoot down a plane.

Man shoots two military recruiters in Little Rock, Arkansas.

Seven North Carolina residents are charged with supporting terrorism and conspiracy to commit murder abroad—one defendant, Daniel Patrick Boyd, had traveled to Pakistan and Afghanistan to train in terrorist camps.

Three men are arrested and charged in an ongoing terror probe in New York and Colorado—one charged with intent to use weapons of mass destruction in New York City.

A Jordanian living in Texas is arrested on charges of intending to bomb a Dallas skyscraper.

A U.S. suspect is arrested and charged with planning to bomb the Springfield, Illinois federal courthouse.

Two men in Chicago are arrested for plotting a terrorist attack on a Danish newspaper (one of the men is later charged with also abetting the November 2008 Mumbai terrorist attack).

Army major kills 13 men and women and wounds over 30 in Fort Hood.

Eight Somali-Americans from Minnesota are charged with terrorism-related counts involving al-Shabaab.

Five men from the Washington, DC area are detained in Pakistan for trying to join militants fighting U.S. troops.

Nigerian Umar Farouk attempts to blow up a Detroit-bound airliner.

The following chart of attack planning by U.S. persons and attack planning against targets on U.S. soil indicates the reach and strength of al-Qa'ida's narrative that has helped inspire individuals to self-radicalize to the point where they are purchasing arms and/or attempting to plan attacks. The dates are displayed according to dates of arrests or indictments. Although there is a spike in 2009, this year may not be an outlier but instead an indicator of plotters who were arrested then but who began their planning in previous years. The chart illustrates al-Qa'ida's unceasing ability to inspire people thousands of miles away to plan violence in the name of al-Qa'ida:

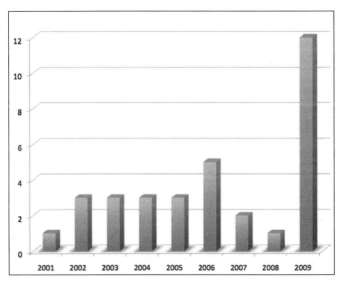

U.S. person attack plans and attack plans against targets on U.S. soil, 2001–2009.

Another example of the reach of al-Qa`ida's marketing lies in the effectiveness of online al-Qa`ida-supporter Anwar al-Awlaki.[13] He openly praises al-

---

[13] In April 2010, Awlaki formally aligned himself with Al-Qa`ida in the Arabian Peninsula with an official Al-Qa`ida in the Arabian Peninsula video—shown on al-Jazira television. However, his apparent global influence as an English-language radicalizer eclipses his position in any radical group. His potency as a spokesman is greater than as a rank and file al-Qa`ida member. He may have joined with the intent of rewarding himself with greater local protection and greater local legitimacy especially since the U.S. President publicized that Awlaki is an official target of the U.S. government.

Qa`ida and is arguably the most popular and pro-
lific online English-language marketer in the world
today with over 1,000 videos of his lectures on
Youtube.

Mainstream media have claimed that recent terrorist suspects have communicated online
with the New Mexico-born Yemen resident al-
Awlaki. Media have also cited terrorism cases in
which suspects or convicts were in part inspired
by Awlaki's online video lectures.

Cases in which Awlaki or his lectures are
reported to have played some role in the recruitment or radicalization of terrorist suspects or
convicts include:

Faisal Shahzad - Pakistani-American Connecticut
resident who allegedly attempted to detonate a
vehicle-borne improvised explosive device in New
York City's Times Square in May 2010. Was reportedly a "fan and follower" of Awlaki's extremist
online lectures. As of 11 May 2010, there was no
evidence Shahzad had any direct contact with Awlaki.

Sharif Mobley - New Jersey resident and former
U.S. nuclear plant employee is a terrorist suspect
detained in Yemen for apparent al-Qa`ida ties. Ac-
cording to media reports from Yemeni government
information, he was in contact with Awlaki. The
reason for his arrest and the nature and the
length of his online contact has not yet been reported.

Colleen R. LaRose (a.k.a. Fatima LaRose a.k.a.
Jihad Jane) - Tied on 9 March 2010 to a reported

assassination plot against Swedish cartoonist Lars Vilks. Media reports that she exchanged emails with Awlaki.

Umar Farouk - Accused of attempting to blow up an airliner, with nearly 300 persons onboard, near Detroit on 25 December 2009. Under questioning by the FBI, Abdulmutallab has said that he met with Awlaki and senior al-Qaʿida members between August and December 2009. Reportedly, Awlaki may have been involved in some elements of planning and/or may have helped to provide religious justification for the planned attack.[xvii]

Nidal Hasan - Suspected of killing 13 and wounding over 30 in Fort Hood on 5 November 2009. Reportedly, he exchanged up to 20 emails with Awlaki. However, the emails reportedly did not indicate the impending attack at Fort Hood or specific acts of violence.

Mohamoud Hassan - Over 20 Minneapolis residents reportedly have traveled to Somalia to join al-Shabaab over the past two years. According to press reports, one of these residents, Mohamoud Hassan who was reportedly killed in Somalia in September 2009, listened to "Constants on the Path to Jihad" lectures by Awlaki before leaving the United States.

Fort Dix Plotters - Six U.S. citizens plotted to attack soldiers at Fort Dix military base in New Jersey. The FBI arrested them on 8 May 2007, and they were found guilty on charges of conspiracy to harm U.S. military personnel on 22 December 2008. According to court documents,

the suspects are alleged to have been inspired by
Awlaki's online lectures.[xviii]

Toronto 18 - Canadian officials arrested 18 individuals on 2 June 2006 who were reportedly
plotting attacks in Ontario. They were accused of
planning to detonate truck bombs; open small
arms fire on a crowd; take hostages; behead the
Prime Minister; and "storm" the Canadian Broad-
casting Center, Canadian Parliament building,
and Canadian Security Intelligence Service. Ring-
leader Zakaria Amara and 17 other Canadians
reportedly listened to Awlaki's online lectures on
conducting violence against Western governments
before their arrest.

London Subway Bombers - Mohammad Sidique
Khan and Shehzad Tanweer, two of the 7 July
2005 bombers who killed 52 London commuters,
were reportedly linked to a Leeds bookstore displaying recordings of Awlaki's lectures.

     Although online messaging may not have
been the main driver of radicalization in all the
examples mentioned in this chapter, effective
marketing has been the common vein. Furthermore, all these groups and individuals made a
conscious decision to act specifically in the name
of al-Qa`ida because of al-Qa`ida's propaganda
and name branding. Al-Qa`ida's marketing suc-
cess even appears to surpass that of major U.S.
soda companies—al-Qa`ida is not persuading peo-
ple to drink a particular brand of refreshing pop,
but rather to murder and die in its name.

8. AL-QA`IDA'S TARGET AUDIENCE: EVERY MUSLIM

Violent extremists share no common profile. They are poor and rich, young and old, and reflect the diversity of Muslim communities worldwide. This includes those who join terrorist groups as well as those who support them, either aggressively or passively by turning a blind eye. Any counter ideology marketing campaign must therefore target every Muslim or person who contemplates conversion to Islam.

To date, no study can definitively answer the question of what radicalizes a violent extremist. Sociopathic tendencies, identity crisis, social isolation, insanity, broken familial background, repressed sexuality, humiliation, poverty, unemployment, romantic ideals, peer pressure, ignorance, psychological manipulation, criminality, or ideology may play a role in specific cases. But there has not yet appeared any mental, physical, ethnic, spiritual, behavioural, or economic common trend among violent extremists. Some cases involve numerous causes while others appear to be devoid of a clear motivation.

Every year or so a study is published that quickly gains popularity in the U.S. security analytic communities. Although studies, especially those that employ data from new polls, may explain some aspects of violent extremism, none explain radicalization holistically.

Marc Sageman's 2004 *Understanding Terror Networks* states that social networks are key to radicalization.

Robert Pape's 2006 *Dying to Win: The Strategic Logic of Suicide Terrorism* explains that suicide attacks are primarily waged when a nation is invaded.

Alan Krueger's 2007 *What Makes a Terrorist: Economics and the Roots of Terrorism* suggests that terrorists tend to be those who are politically active or interested. Behavior, not demographics, can inform who is more apt to become radicalized.

Colonel John M. Venhaus' (U.S. Army) 2010 *Why Youth Join al-Qaeda* concludes that young people who are attracted to al-Qa`ida's ideology are revenge, status, identity, or thrill seekers, all adolescent developmental features.

However, despite compelling analysis and copious data culling, these four examples offer limited help to counterterrorism analysts. First, none of the studies explains most terrorist attacks. Each attack is waged by a person who normally carries numerous and sometimes contradictory influences and outlooks. Second, the studies simply confirm previous claims by regional experts.

It is clear to any Lance Corporal serving in Afghanistan that terrorists are often urged into violent extremism by groups of friends, family, or other communities. And groups use suicide bombers as a tactical option when wealthier nations invade poorer ones, and not on account of some innate masochistic suicidal tendency. Furthermore, terrorists will often begin as activists or those who aspire to be activists.

These and other studies are helpful and even informed this book. However, none of the studies answers the question of what radicalizes a violent extremist. And none can help identify someone susceptible to violent extremism.

Before continuing, it is important to dispel popular misconceptions that poverty, ungoverned areas, and repression could be drivers of radicalization. These popular notions are fallacy. If poverty were a radicalization driver, why are most Chinese and those in poor sections of El Salvador not conducting suicide attacks? If repression were a driver of radicalization, then why do we not see similar trends in North Korea and Cuba? And if ungoverned areas were a driver, then why do we not see radicalization in outlying areas of Mongolia and Patagonia? In fact, the vast majority of terrorist attacks over the last 16 months have had nothing to do with poverty, lawless areas, or repression.

Most violent extremists are wealthy, educated, and have access to freedoms—more so than most in the world. In most cases, people who are poor and looking for potable water and food simply have pressing life-saving concerns that preclude the luxury of picking up arms in the name of al-Qa`ida. But despite evidence and logic, even the U.S. Secretary of State, in several 2009 speeches, wrongly insinuated a connection between poverty and extremism.

Study and after study indicates no such association. Poverty, ungoverned areas, and repression are not drivers of radicalization. So at least we know not to focus anti-al-Qa`ida efforts solely on impoverished, ungoverned, or repressed communities.

The following studies are just a small sample disproving connections between poverty and al-Qa`ida's violent extremism:

- A 2006 Gallup World Poll of over 9,000 interviews in nine predominantly Muslim countries found that violent extremism-supporting Muslims are more likely to be wealthy and to have stayed in school longer than "moderates."

- In Marc Sageman's 2004 study of 132 terrorists, over 60 percent had some college education and 4 percent had a doctoral degree, making this sample pool more educated than most in the third world.[xix]

- Netherlands Institute of International Relations' Dr. Edwin Bakker's 2006 study of 242 European violent extremists concluded that socioeconomic background and criminal history of terrorists are similar to backgrounds of young persons in immigrant Muslim communities in Europe.[xx]

- In a sample of 232 Arab suicide attackers associated with Lebanon, Palestine, and al-Qa`ida from 1980–2003, Robert Pape found that religiously driven suicide bombers had similar education levels and socioeconomic status to the Palestinian and Lebanese publics.[xxi]

- Israeli Defense Forces Lieutenant Colonel Anat Berko concluded, from interviews with Palestinian suicide bomber dispatchers and failed suicide attackers, that many terrorists did not have financial difficulties. She found that attackers who failed in carrying out their missions held a standard of living comparable with most Palestinians.[xxii]

- Professor Steffen Hertog at Paris' Science Po found that cognitive factors could be the reason for the abundance of educated engineers in violent extremist organizations. In a talk at the Carnegie Endowment for International Peace in September 2009, Hertog stated, based on a varied sample of violent extremist groups, that members were four times as likely to have upper-level education as the general population from which members came. Among samples of violent extremists, approximately 44 percent had engineering backgrounds. Among the more educated, engineers are three times as likely to embrace violent extremist groups as other upper-level graduates. According to Hertog, there is no supporting evidence for the claim that engineers are recruited for their technical skills.

- Colonel John M. Venhaus (U.S. Army), from 2,303 interviews and personal histories of violent extremists, drew the conclusion that "[a]lthough radical Islamic ideologies use the rhetoric of economic oppression to enhance their argument, their subjects are generally not drawn from the ranks of the desperately poor."[xxiii]

Anecdotal evidence suggests that some mainstream Muslims could even turn to violence while seeking an education in a place with opportunity, freedom, political expression, and wealth. Sayyid Qutb's (modern extremism's "godfather") education exchange in the United States led him to despise what he perceived as the West's immorality. His observations while a student in the United States sparked the prelude to his later journey into radicalism after he returned home to Egypt.

Other anecdotal evidence of wealthy individuals with access to social mobility includes the most notorious terrorist of the twentieth century, Khalid al-Islambuli. In broad daylight, Islambuli brazenly assassinated President of Egypt Anwar Sadat while Sadat was making an appearance on television. As a military officer, he arguably had more options, respect, and social mobility than professors, engineers, and lawyers in 1980s Egypt. However, when his brother was dragged out of his family's house in his pajamas as part of a countrywide roundup of suspected militants, Islambuli was enraged and ready to kill.[xxiv] Islambuli was not a brainwashed or blind follower of some ideal or some dynamic leader, but a young man who independently waged a violent act over a personal grudge. He devised the plan and recruited his accomplices on his own to kill Sadat and destroy the government. This was not a top-down operation. Islambuli got approval and ideological sanction from extremist leadership, single-handedly finagled his armed accomplices onto a parade vehicle, and accomplished one of the most infamous attacks of any militant group in the twentieth century. Islambuli and his accomplices in broad daylight fired on government and military leaders, killing Sadat. The only reason why so many officials were spared was that many of the grenades were inoperable.

Further examples of relatively privileged terrorists include U.S. Army major Nidal Hassan, alleged to have shot innocents at Fort Hood in November 2009; Umar Farouk, son of one of the wealthiest Nigerian bankers, who attempted to down an airliner near Detroit in December 2010; and Connecticut-resident Faisal Shahzad, who attempted to kill civilians in Times Square in May 2010.

Al-Qa`ida appears to understand that violent extremists come from an array of backgrounds. Therefore, al-Qa`ida targets all Muslim communities with its online messaging with the hope of reaching someone, anyone. Likewise, any competing narrative campaign must target Muslims as widely as possible.

9. AL-QA`IDA'S IDEOLOGY: VIOLENCE, ONLY VIOLENCE, NOTHING BUT VIOLENCE

As mentioned in the definitions section of the book, al-Qa`ida comprises hidden leaders who inspire others to conduct violent attacks in its name. Whenever news reports broadcast that al-Qa`ida is bankrupt or physically isolated, the information is meaningless in assessing al-Qa`ida's potency. The very nature of al-Qa`ida is that the core leaders are inspirers and not active militants. They *do not need* money, ammunition, or freedom of movement as long as they are able to get their message out on the Internet to inspire others to do their fighting.

This message which is promoted from computer screens is hinged on an obsession with violence as the one and only way to gain an international caliphate. To understand the level of dedication to violence and complete disregard for all other tactics such as diplomacy, education, politics, or Ghandi-style active civil disobedience, one must understand the descent into raw brutality al-Qa`ida took in the decades leading up to its inception.

One major factor that has a prime influence on al-Qa`ida is the pool of Egyptian militants and ideologues from the twentieth century. To understand al-Qa`ida ideology, one must investigate Egyptian violent extremist ideology.

Al-Qa`ida's leadership core comprises a

plurality of Egyptians. Although Usama bin Ladin is a Saudi of Yemeni dissent, his core group of lieutenants and most influential ideologues (past and present) are Egyptians who are an extension of the Egyptian Islamic Jihad (EIJ). Ayman al-Zawahiri (chief lieutenant), Mustafa Abu al-Yazid (reportedly killed in 2010 and former head financier and Taliban liaison), Saif Al-Adel (reportedly a member of the Egyptian Islamic Jihad around the time of Sadat's assassination), and Abu Khabab al-Masri (a.k.a. Midhat Mursi al-Sayid Uma, the deceased head bomb maker) are just four examples of Egyptians in al-Qa`ida's top echelon. But of greater importance is the central role of Egyptian ideology on al-Qa`ida's violent nature today.

Al-Qa`ida is an amalgamation of varying ideological influences to include inspirations from the Indian subcontinent, Palestine, and Saudi Arabia. However, the most enduring influences are Egyptian. Therefore, to understand al-Qa`ida, its ideology, and why it assumes that only violence is the solution to creating some sort of undefined caliphate, one must understand the nature of the descent into militancy of the Egyptians who comprise al-Qa`ida's inner core—former members of the now defunct EIJ.

Quick History of the EIJ

The EIJ was a militant Muslim Brotherhood off-shoot, which decided that only violent overthrow of the Egyptian government would produce a state as God intended. They chose violence because past political and social activism landed previous students and Muslim Brotherhood groups in prison or on death row.

EIJ militants in Cairo failed to overthrow the government (as they intended) after Islambuli's team assassinated President Sadat in 1981. A simultaneous rebellion of Upper Egypt cells lasted less than 24 hours. After some leaders were jailed or executed, other leaders and militants fled to Pakistan, where they chose the official name "Egyptian Islamic Jihad," and then fled to Sudan.

The EIJ attempted to assassinate the Interior and Prime Ministers in 1993, bombed the Egyptian Embassy in Islamabad in 1995, and planned an attack against the U.S. Embassy in Albania in 1998. In 1998, the EIJ leadership partnered with Usama Bin Ladin. In 2001, the EIJ officially fused with al-Qa`ida.[xxv]

The following are some of al-Qa`ida's key Egyptian influences:

Hasan al-Banna (1906–1949)

Muslim Brotherhood founder Hasan al-Banna, whom the British-backed monarchy executed in 1949, sowed the seeds for future generations to struggle to create an undefined super-nation that would abide by an un-described interpretation of religious law, a goal that EIJ and then al-Qa`ida would adopt. Al-Banna wished to liberate Muslims, in Egypt and ultimately all countries, from foreign and secular rule and influence, and then establish an umbrella Islamic state.

He spoke of a slow evolution beginning with each individual and ending with governments, perhaps lasting generations. Al-Banna believed that only Islam and its laws could solve all social, political, and economic problems, although he never described exactly how Islam would solve these challenges.[xxvi]

EIJ members grew up with al-Banna's theories. Even today, he is cited in al-Qa'ida texts.

Sayyid Qutb (1906–1966)

Brotherhood member and al-Banna doctrine pupil Sayyid Qutb wove a violent thread into al-Banna's patient vision. Qutb eventually inspired future EIJ members with his written attacks on the Egyptian regime, eschewing all secularism, even Nasser's Arabism which ruled at the end of Qutb's life.

Qutb dispensed with al-Banna's vision for a slow personal evolution toward a new society. He replaced al-Banna's vision of personal evolution with a desire to overtake the government as soon as possible.

Originally, however, Qutb was part of the regime he eventually grew to hate. He consulted for the Revolutionary Command Council whose members were socialist military officers who toppled Egypt's British-backed monarchy in 1952. At the time, the Command Council partnered with the Muslim Brotherhood to buy greater societal backing. The Brotherhood's social programs, such as food and housing for the needy, were wildly popular. At this early period in his career, Qutb expressly thought his religion could apply to modern government as it was at that time, expressly secular.[xxvii]

Qutb's moderate journey stopped abruptly when the government turned on the Brotherhood two years into its reign. Following a possibly staged and overly dramatized (on radio) assassination attempt on the President, the government burned down the Muslim Brotherhood headquarters and arrested and tortured its leaders and followers, including Qutb.[xxviii] Security forces rounded up towns worth of males, such as a Brotherhood stronghold in Kardasa near Cairo. After allowing the Muslim Brotherhood a two-year taste of power, Nasser stomped out any hopes of political aspirations and forced Qutb to question the core belief of al-Banna's slow evolutionary strategy.

Qutb's world was jolted further in prison, where he gained the voice that would help spur EIJ and then al-Qa`ida to violence. After prison guards killed twenty-one protesting Brothers, forcing the wounded inmates to die in place, Qutb concluded the government and all its members were godless and unrighteous.[xxix]

Qutb then wrote his seminal *Milestones* to call all Muslims to destroy the secular government and to adhere strictly to religious law, without any legislation or debate. (He failed to define specifically his interpretation of what religious law meant or how exactly it should be applied.) Qutb stated that laws from people were inherently flawed because people are imperfect. Thus, man-made laws would inevitably fail:

*...all manmade individual or collective theo-
ries have proved to be failures...It is
necessary to revive that Muslim community
which is buried under the debris of the
manmade traditions of several generations,
and which is crushed under the weight of
those false laws and customs which are not
even remotely related to the Islamic teachings, and which, in spite of all this, calls
itself the 'world of Islam.'*xxx

Like many of those who would comprise
EIJ and later al-Qa`ida's leadership, Qutb was
radicalized by repression and torture. It was not
some personally driven philosophical shift. The
fear of torture, which he and his friends suffered,
sparked the harshness of *Milestones*. Qutb's book,
however, might not have been revenge so much as
an awakening in him to a realization that only violence could achieve al-Banna's original goal of an
Islamic state.

Foreseeing Qutb as a future and powerful
martyr and predicting future generations of "Qut-
bists," Nasser sent Vice President Sadat in person
to offer reconciliation and the post of Minister of
Education to Qutb. Qutb refused and died.xxxi His
1966 execution sealed the legacy of his ideas for
future EIJ members. Militants wept his martyrdom and adhered to his harsh narrative of the
need to overthrow the government.

A young generation of students and work-
ers, those who would comprise the EIJ and
eventually the al-Qa`ida core, diverged from the
political base of the Brothers. This new generation
relished *Milestones*, as evidenced in student

meetings and publications of the late 1960s. In 1966, future EIJ leader Ayman al-Zawahiri, his younger brother, and classmates made a pact to oppose the Egyptian government in line with Qutb's views.[xxxii]

Qutb also began a modern extremist tradition of those without religious training reducing rich religious texts and ideologies into easy-to-understand populist propaganda. Suddenly, theories of jihad, which once were stuck in the libraries of inaccessible universities, were at the fingertips of Muslims everywhere and were made relevant for the contemporary man. For *Milestones*, he drew in large part on texts written by Ibn Tayimiyya, who was a 13th/14th century prisoner who called for the violent toppling of the Mongols and all Arab entities that supported or did not fight the intruders.

To this day, al-Qa`ida has excelled at marketing complicated ideas in easily digestible short manuscripts for the average person. Counter-al-Qa`ida ideologues, however, offer texts that are typically long-winded and steeped in scholarly language, reason, and nuanced assessments of Islam's original documents. In short, Qutb inspired generations of marketers to come.

Abd-al-Salam Faraj (1952–1982)

Faraj was an author, ideologue, and chief of the first iteration of Islamic Jihad, which later officially became the "Egyptian Islamic Jihad" when it moved to Pakistan and had to differentiate its name from other terrorist groups. (For the sake of simplicity, I will refer to the group as the EIJ in each of its phases.) The Egyptian government swiftly executed Faraj and the team of assassins after Sadat was assassinated in a public shooting.

Faraj strove to further erase uncertainty and hesitancy over the importance of destroying the regime. In his treatise *Hidden Imperative*, Faraj put EIJ's strategy into words. He defined the enemy, refuted strategies of earlier Egyptian militant groups, and explained his rules of warfare.[xxxiii] He was bent on success and seemed besieged and even sanctimonious in his dedication to overturning the government violently and immediately. Faraj, more clearly than Qutb or any other ideologue, defined why EIJ and then al-Qa`ida would be blindly bent on violence alone as the path to achieve political goals. Faraj expressed the extreme nature of EIJ and al-Qa`ida better than any other author. I recommend that any student of al-Qa`ida or counterterrorism read Faraj's treatise.

Unlike Qutb, Faraj was not an innovative marketer. Instead, he was able to put into words the feelings of militant movements already growing in Egypt's underground. He was ultimately speaking to the already converted: disenchanted students and former Brotherhood affiliates and sympathizers already ready for violence. What makes Faraj special in the context of Egypt in the late 1970s is that he put into words what others were feeling.

In *Hidden Imperative*, Faraj was consumed with peaceful movements' lack of success. Failure of the moderate Muslim Brotherhood, jama'at islamiyya (student association), and other religiously inspired groups shaped Faraj's treatise. Faraj's dispensing with any peaceful consideration foretells EIJ and then al-Qa`ida's absolute refusal to consider any type of reconciliation or negotiation.[xxxiv] Specifically, Faraj argued away every strategy of earlier unsuccessful government opponents:

- Muslim charitable organizations lacked the weapons and will to overthrow a regime.

- Islamist political parties were not changing governance; they were actually partaking in and strengthening the very apostate government they sought to discredit.

- Entering government service, rising in the ranks, and taking over state authority from the inside was counterproductive. Participation in state government would only strengthen government institutions, independent of intended outcome.

- Reliance on simple calls to religion would shift precious assets to an effort whose goal would not directly bring an end to the government.

- Newspaper and radio efforts to urge a coup would inevitably fail because the government controlled the media.[xxxv]

- Emigrating abroad to construct an army to return later to face the regime would expose humiliating cowardice and fear of the regime—granting the regime confidence.[xxxvi]

- Devotion to study alone would needlessly delay the violence required to topple the government.[xxxvii]

- Fighting colonialist regimes abroad would allow the apostate power at home to grow stronger without its opposition present.[xxxviii]

All these strategies would fail in Faraj's opinion and had led to prison and/or execution in twentieth century Egypt. Faraj believed that violence was not only necessary tactically, but a requirement of God—the sixth pillar of Islam.

According to Faraj, mainstream religious scholars neglected violence in the name of religion when it should be obligatory for all Muslims to establish an Islamic state. Decades later, this same sentiment has been echoed in every speech from the mouths of al-Qa`ida ideologues and supporters. Faraj wrote: "There is no doubt that the idols of this world can only be made to disappear through the power of the sword."[xxxix]

To Faraj, President Sadat's (who took over after Nasser died in 1970) application of human laws was as appalling as the Mongols' reign of power in the thirteenth century. Unlike non-Muslim regimes, Muslim leaders were held to greater account by Faraj for they could not hide behind a curtain of unreligious ignorance.[xl] Just as Ibn Tayimmiya targeted the Mongols' puppets for obligatory attack, Faraj encouraged Sadat's end: "...A group of people who refuse to carry out part of the clear and reliably transmitted duties of Islam have to be fought..."[xli]

Central to his ideology, and that of the EIJ and later al-Qa`ida, Faraj justified takfir, labeling Muslim unbelievers to justify the killing of these Muslims as religiously permissible. This controversial tactic would open Faraj and Faraj's followers and successors to verbal attack by governments and religious scholars the world over. Criticisms rang out that Faraj and his devotees lacked the requisite understanding of Islam's texts to determine someone an unbeliever.

Even Sheikh Abdallah Azzam, bin Ladin's Palestinian associate during the war against Russia in Afghanistan, challenged EIJ's justification over takfir and targeting of Muslim governments. Fortunately for Faraj's legacy, a car bomb killed Azzam in 1989. With the internal assassination of Azzam, EIJ members persuaded bin Ladin to target Muslim governments. The Egyptians won this ideological fight, perhaps with TNT in lieu of a better argument.

Faraj's failure was his mistaken faith that only a small cell of a dedicated few would be able to take power in Egypt with great speed and deadly force.[xlii] This failed tactic played out after Sadat's 1981 assassination, which failed to inspire a major uprising in Cairo and ignited only a one-day-long rebellion in Upper Egypt.

EIJ wanted to replicate the spirit of the Iranian revolution of 1979 and even the seemingly popular uprising of Nasser and his secularist free officer movement in 1952. (The public in actuality had little to do with the 1952 revolution.) But in the case of Egypt in 1981, the government did not hesitate to arrest entire male populations of towns and kill as many as possible to put down rumors of rebellion, including executing potentially compromised members of police and military units. Those that were most loyal to Sadat enjoyed greater benefits than the rest of the citizenry and ran every important economic, cultural, and governmental position from universities to the press. The rulers had every incentive to stay in power and would kill to maintain their positions.[xliii]

The bottom line was that Egypt was not a good target for Faraj. And Faraj's failed uprising may be largely why al-Qa`ida does not directly attack superior forces or attempt residence in tightly governed areas today.

Dr. Fadl (b. 1950)

Faraj was the ideologue that defined EIJ in broad terms as a group dedicated only to violence, while Dr. Fadl was the practical manager who oversaw its organizational growth that eventually led to a marriage with al-Qa`ida.

Government retribution after the 1981 attack was so vast and harsh that the EIJ was forced to move to Pakistan. Sayyid Imam al-Sharif (a.k.a. Dr. Fadl), the man who officially dubbed the organization "Egyptian Islamic Jihad" in 1987, took the helm.[xliv] He led a newly radicalized group of militants fresh from Egypt's most notorious prisons.

Up until fall of 2007, Fadl was internationally renowned for penning the violent extremist "bible" and al-Qa`ida playbook *Foundations of the Preparations for Jihad* on top of a body of literature providing theological guidance, organizational recommendations, and tactical lessons for violent extremists worldwide.[xlv] U.S. Military Academy's Combating Terrorism Center assesses that ideologically Fadl is as influential as Usama bin Ladin.[xlvi] Former EIJ associate Montasser Al-Zayyat maintains that Fadl was EIJ's theological core even more so than Faraj had been, but this claim cannot be confirmed.[xlvii]

As he volunteered his days in a Peshawar hospital, Fadl shelled out execution sentences by night for Muslims who did not abide by EIJ principles. He tirelessly oversaw publication of the monthly magazine "The Conquest" and became the prosecutor and judge of a "takfiri court" where he ordered executions for wayward mujahidin. One guilty defendant was found in the streets sliced to pieces as a warning to others.[xlviii]

He wrote articles that would spell out how to create cells and plan attacks for a worldwide generation of militants to come. He also sat alongside his successor, Ayman al-Zawahiri, on a leadership council advising the up-and-coming wealthy Usama bin Ladin.

In 1993, Fadl fled Peshawar to Sudan, and then Yemen in the throws of civil war. Famous for being a frontline warrior, and despite his infamy and power as head of the EIJ, he returned to the field as a volunteer physician in Yemeni hospitals to help those wounded in the civil war.[xlix]

Although his resignation may have been a symptom of internal power maneuvers or the new wife he found in Yemen, Fadl today claims his mindset turned less militant a year before his EIJ retirement.

Dr. Fadl's resignation and subsequent capture years later would allow his successor's complete convergence with al-Qa`ida.

Ayman al-Zawahiri (b. 1951)

Like many other EIJ leaders, Zawahiri suffered inhumane torture that would shape his extremist career. As a child in a wealthy home and neighborhood, Zawahiri was known to obsess over poetry and Disney films and to avoid the local sports club because he thought wrestling and boxing were inhumane.[1] But this disposition began to change in young adulthood. Swayed, in part, by his activist uncle who was a close Sayyid Qutb confidant,[li] Zawahiri reportedly helped in the weapons smuggling that would arm the failed post-Sadat-assassination coup. For his participation in the failed coup, Zawahiri was arrested in a 1981 crackdown.

In prison, he spoke directly to the media on behalf of inmates who had been tortured. According to his story, hungry dogs would come into his cell when he was tied up and have their way. Zawahiri yelled to the press, "They shocked us with electricity. And they used the wild dogs. And they used the wild dogs."[lii] According to journalist Lawrence Wright, it is common practice for Egyptian guards to tie a prisoner backwards to a chair and force abused or drugged dogs to rape the inmate.[liii]

Security forces compelled Zawahiri to entrap and identify an extremist mentor, close friend, and EIJ cell commander, Major Qamari, leading to Qamari's imprisonment and death. To cause further discontent, prison guards threw Qamari (while he was alive) and Zawahiri into the same cell.[liv] This physical and psychological torture likely helped push Zawahiri to take on Faraj's absolute devotion to violence, with no consideration for politics or negotiation.

During the war in Afghanistan, Zawahiri treated Usama bin Ladin medically and used this close personal relationship to persuade bin Ladin to appoint EIJ members to key posts in bin Ladin's better-funded organization.[lv]

EIJ unraveled when the Egyptian government discovered a computer holding EIJ identities that led to 800 arrests in Egypt in the early 1990s. Then, 1993's failed assassination attempt on the prime minister left a schoolgirl dead and enraged Egyptians, stripping the EIJ of any remnant of popular empathy and providing security forces with greater determination.

Organizational bankruptcy forced Zawahiri in 1995 to ask EIJ members to donate their own salaries to continue operations. Lack of funds also forced Zawahiri to follow the rich bin Ladin to Sudan and then back to Afghanistan again.[lvi]

Egypt had become so dangerous that Zawahiri could not return to seek more recruits and financing. At this point, EIJ had no reprieve save joining al-Qa`ida. In 1998, Zawahiri signed EIJ into a unified movement with bin Ladin. In 2001, EIJ was completely incorporated into Al-Qa`ida. EIJ took the key ideological and command posts and used lessons learned from its history, especially its mistakes with regard to confronting Egypt's government head-on with a coup, to design an al-Qa`ida that would use safe havens and spread its narrative internationally to inspire others to do its bidding.

More than any other influence, al-Qa`ida assumed EIJ's ideology of "violence is the only answer," regardless of innocent Muslim victims, theological unsoundness, and strategic illogic.

10. SOLUTION: IDENTIFY, TRANSLATE, EMPOWER MUSLIM VOICES

Al-Qa`ida is well aware of its leaders' mortality, the limits of physical isolation, and the importance of inspiring others to keep the movement alive. Therefore, it focuses primarily on marketing its narrative to inspire others to do its bidding, while counter al-Qa`ida voices remain mute. These counter narratives are not translated and rarely available on the Internet. And they lack the layperson accessibility and populist flare of their extremist counterparts.

To destroy al-Qa`ida for good, its main strength, popular support, must be severed completely. An effort must be made to drive an irreparable wedge between violent extremists and nonviolent Muslims so that recruitment pools and support dry up. Then, the hardened unrehabilitatable militants will be isolated and left to die.

Some level of societal support is al-Qa`ida's lifeblood. Even at the most visceral level, Muslim suicide attackers rely on some semblance of public approval in order to muster up the will to make the ultimate sacrifice. Suicide bombers seek death specifically because at least parts of some Muslim communities venerate the sacrifice. Without acceptance, if terrorists are ineligible for martyrdom status in any of the world's Muslim communities, recruits will less likely be willing to die in the name of God.

To isolate al-Qa`ida and even inspire social movements to revolt against al-Qa`ida, I propose a strategy to identify, translate, and amplify persuasive and independent counter-al-Qa`ida messages onto a robust network of easily searchable websites in numerous languages.

I propose using al-Qa`ida's techniques to help inspire a counter-al-Qa`ida revolution.

11. IDENTIFYING THE MESSAGE

Authors of persuasive counter-al-Qa`ida messages are popularly considered independent of governments, especially secular Arab, E.U., and U.S. governments. Their arguments use reason, emotion, and religious grounding to undermine al-Qa`ida and al-Qa`ida-affiliate justifications for violence.

Counter-al-Qa`ida writers, to be effective, will normally be anti-United States, anti-Israel, anti-West, and even anti-democracy. Such views are necessary evils and often the only way for speakers and writers to claim independence from the West and Western allies to maintain credibility.

Arguments will not contest al-Qa`ida's claim for the need to defend Islam against the West. This would be playing into al-Qa`ida's popular narrative and essentially arguing on al-Qa`ida's terms. Instead, they will focus on the heresy and practical limitations of al-Qa`ida violence. These messages are found in local, national, and international newspapers, online media sources, published books, popular English academic and policy journals, independent websites, blogs, and online social media.

When searching for a message to amplify, there are two major factors to consider: the message and the messenger. The best-case scenario—

a message that has the best chance to resonate— is a message that is itself persuasive and comes from the mouth or pen of someone who commands respect. But there exist shades of gray from this level of perfection that may still enjoy success.

A powerful message that uses strong humanitarian and religious verbiage may be powerful from an anonymous blogger. A weak message, poorly worded without focus from a respected religious leader or a person who won fame on a battlefield, may still resound somewhat due to the known credentials of the messenger.

But someone tainted by government affiliation with a message that is inane will unlikely persuade anyone.

One cannot rely purely on one factor or the other. Instead, one must look for a balance. There will never be the perfect message, perfect in substance and in the reputation of the speaker or author.

Studying the potential of a message is akin to studying Hadith in Islamic studies. Each Hadith (action or saying of the Prophet transmitted from person to person from the first generation orally until it was written down centuries later) stands on the matn (substance of the account) and isnad (chain of transmitters). To this day, Western and non-Western scholars debate the validity and importance of each of the thousands of Hadith through analysis of the account itself, reputation of the transmitters, and circumstances of each individual transmission.

A strong Hadith will have an unbroken chain of transmitters, each with an impeccable reputation for piety and intelligence, and a story or saying that makes sense in the context and spirit of what the Prophet did and taught. Some scholars have whittled accoptablc/valid Hadith to fewer than a dozen in number. Others argue for a hundred or thousands to be accepted. The scholarship and debate over Hadith will never die. Likewise, study and arguments over which messages may best undermine al-Qa`ida will never end. But in both cases, we strive to find the best messages and the best messengers.

An example of a message that would likely fail is Yemen foreign minister Abu-Bakr al-Qirbi's October 2009 statement against al-Qa`ida. The message is powerful and has the potential to persuade. However, the messenger himself (a member of an opaque government that has worked closely with the United States) seems more bent on survival than upholding religious or humanitarian ideals. Al-Qirbi said:

> *We know that there are al-Qa`ida members [in Yemen] and that there are threats, but this activity is aimed at soft targets and innocent victims through bombings, regrettably.*

> *Al-Qa`ida lost much of its standing because the people who thought that it would confront what they term (the Zionist and American) enemy, realized that it, in fact, harmed only Islam and the Muslims, and that it killed only their brothers in Islam.*

> *Look at the victims whom we see in the*

hundreds in Iraq, Pakistan, Afghanistan, and other countries. These groups remain a danger with which we must deal. Praise be to God, the Yemeni security agencies managed to close in on them, and they will continue to do so until victory over these groups has been achieved.

Al-Qirbi's statement is potentially, at first look, an effective counter narrative. He explains that al-Qa`ida targets civilians as clearly shown by Muslims dead in Afghanistan, Pakistan, and Iraq. Al-Qa`ida has failed to deliver on its promises to confront the United States and Israel, and al-Qa`ida damages the very institution of Islam itself. In short, al-Qirbi attempts to close the distance between al-Qa`ida death-making abroad and his countrymen, few of whom have experienced al-Qa`ida violent tactics firsthand.

Although the message includes vital elements of a potentially successful counter narrative, the messenger, who is a prominent member of the Yemeni government, undermined this particular statement. Al-Qa`ida and most Yemenis carry a general disdain for central authority, which is a main theme al-Qa`ida in the Arabian Peninsula exploits. Many Yemenis view the Yemeni government as authoritarian and corrupt. Despite a fair election, the government is run without transparency by a tribe surrounding President Salih, much as Saddam Hussein ruled (minus the level of crimes against humanity). Yemenis believe that security forces work too closely with distrusted outside forces on counterterrorism issues, namely the U.S. government.

In conclusion, few Yemenis will be inspired outright by al-Qirbi's statement because of his position as a government official and lack of independence.

The same message from an independent source would be more influential and could potentially compete with al-Qa`ida in the Arabian Peninsula's narrative.

It is tempting to write a chart with messenger credentials on the X axis and message substance on the Y axis to determine overall potential effectives, as characters in the film *Dead Poets Society* do in their too-simplistic "greatness-of-a-poem chart." But as with determining the greatness of a poem, there is no science and no numerical value attached to a message. Any attempt is folly.

At the end of the day, the potential power of a message is a qualitative judgment weighing sometimes hundreds of factors. Practically speaking, this will mean throwing "good enough" messages at audiences and then seeing which ones gain traction (more on measurements of success later). Just as al-Qa`ida delivers hundreds of messages per year, some even clearly contradictory, without worry over getting messages crossed and confused, a counter-narrative campaign should not be too tied up with trying to amplify "perfect" messages.

There is no "perfect" message. However, there are narratives with good substance from reputable sources that may persuade.

Finally, it should be added that in rare cases an "unbalanced" message, in which either the substance or the narrator lacks the potential to inspire, may still have some sort of effect. For example, if a religious leader pens an anti-al-Qa`ida document with weak and scattered arguments (these are out there—more on this later), an al-Qa`ida spokesman may still react. Basically, if confused as to whether to amplify a message or not, one should maintain bias for action.

The anti-al-Qa`ida message may be so badly written that al-Qa`ida leaders could consider the message an easy low-hanging fruit to refute. If al-Qa`ida falls for this trap, it is wasting its time and giving more credence than the original anti-al-Qa`ida message may deserve. Bad publicity is publicity nonetheless.

12. THE MESSENGER: THE OVERT HAND OF GOVERNMENT IS THE KISS OF DEATH

The most effective messengers against a group like al-Qa`ida may be religious leaders, former violent extremists, or victims.

Religious leaders, if they have a following, religious training, and practice, may possess greater credentials than al-Qa`ida and its affiliate ideologues with their questionable religious status.

Former violent extremists who are newly reformed carry the same battlefield scars, romantic war stories, and legends as their still extremist contemporaries and can impress the same battle-hungry or battle-curious youth.

Victims of al-Qa`ida vividly underline al-Qa`ida's violent ideology that allows it to execute wanton tatarrus.

RELIGIOUS LEADERS

Two obstacles may impede the ability of religious leaders to persuade Muslims to oppose al-Qa`ida. First, many Muslim-majority countries' top Muslim scholars and prayer leaders have deep ties to the state. Examples are Saudi and Egyptian clergy whom respective citizens accuse of close collaboration with heads of state with the mission of vocally justifying state initiatives and heeding government orders to promote government legitimacy. Therefore, the task of identifying respected, seasoned, and schooled scholars who are also assumed to be independent of government influence will be a challenge. Complete independence may be impossible.

Second, al-Qa`ida and its supporters often portray themselves as strict constructionists, deemed "Salafis." They believe modern man should do away with generations of labored scholarship over the original texts of Islam and religious law. Al-Qa`ida states that it prefers to refer directly to the original doctrines without the stain of human interpretation which is inherently imperfect. Some even outwardly shun the four major schools of Sunni thought—each predicated with a methodology to interpret Islamic texts. Therefore, as much as possible, Salafi scholars are needed in an attempt to delegitimize and dissuade other Salafis who may have the propensity to support al-Qa`ida in the future.

The following are examples who have provided effective counter narratives that should be translated and amplified worldwide. These examples also illustrate the types of persons or groups of people to identify in future attempts to discredit and inspire revolt against violent transnational insurrections.

Salman al-Awdah

Former Usama bin Ladin mentor and reformed violent extremist ideologue Salman al-Awdah's

English and Arabic counter narratives continue to have the potential to delegitimize al-Qa`ida. However, al-Awdah's narratives suffer from limited readership. Because of his former extremist credentials, religious training, and continual shows of public respect for Usama bin Ladin, al-Awdah continues to be an enduring competing voice that has the potential to put violent extremists on the defensive.

Also, the immaculate English translations of al-Awdah's press releases and letters help to reach a diverse though small audience from Malaysia to Pakistan to Canada, underlining the importance of professional translation of competing narratives to have any effect on diverse audiences.

On 15 November 2009, al-Awdah released a condemnation of the Fort Hood shooting. He stated that the incident might make those in the U.S. military question the intentions of other Muslims. He also said, "This action taken out by Nidal Hasan was irrational and is empty of thought..."

More popular still is al-Awdah's 2007 open letter to Usama bin Ladin criticizing al-Qa`ida violence and killing of innocent civilians. This message, still available on his website Islamtoday.com and other blogs and online articles, includes the following statements:[lvii]

> *How much blood has been spilled? How many innocent children, women, and old people have been killed, maimed, and expelled from their homes in the name of 'al-Qa`ida'?*

Are you happy to meet Allah with this heavy burden on your shoulders? It is a weighty burden indeed—at least hundreds of thousands of innocent people, if not millions.

How could you wish for that?—after knowing that Allah's Messenger said: 'Whoever as much as kills a sparrow in vain will find it crying before Allah on the Day of Judgment: My Lord! That person killed me in vain. He did not kill me for needful sustenance.'

This religion of ours comes to defense of the life of a sparrow. It can never accept the murder of innocent people, regardless of what supposed justification is given for it.

Al-Awdah's website Islamtoday.com is not ranked on popular free website monitoring services, which indicates a relatively low viewership. Of the website's few visitors, 17.4 percent are from Pakistan, 14.8 percent from India, 12.8 percent from Indonesia, 12.0 percent from the United States, 6 percent from the United Kingdom, and the rest from Egypt, Malaysia, Mauritius, Canada, Morocco, and other countries.[lviii]

Al-Awdah is reputable. His message is sound. But he lacks al-Qa`ida's worldwide media network. Thus, al-Awdah's message remains muted—when compared to al-Qa`ida's messaging—to much of the Muslim world.

Mohammed El Fazazi

In July 2009, German media broke the story of a letter renouncing violence from formerly revered violent extremist preacher Mohammed El Fazazi.[lix] El Fazazi wrote the letter to his daughter who lives in Hamburg. In the letter, Fazazi states that he has been imprisoned unjustly for the past six years in Morocco, he is not an extremist, and immigrants in Germany should act peacefully. He concludes his letter with a defense of the German government as an entity that protects Muslims and religious freedoms.

The following are translations of counter-violence excerpts from El Fazazi's letter:

> *...I, Muhammad bin Muhammad El Fazazi, the writer of these lines, have not been forced to put these down. I am under no pressure to write this...*
>
> *And those who don't want anything but killing, blood, robbery and theft have nothing to do with the religion of Allah the Exalted.*
>
> *Ahd Iman, a security contract [in reference to contracts German immigrants sign] for both sides and Allah says in his beloved book: 'You who have given security, keep the contracts.' So it follows that anything that breaks these contracts—e.g. by declaring theft to be permitted, or by allowing the killing of the population in the name of jihad, or by trying to build cells who put people into a state of fear and horror and so on—in my*

eyes constitutes a breach of contract and be-
trayal in regard to what one has signed in
the embassy, in the consulate or in the im-
migration office.

It is the job of immigrants to debate and en-
gage...by means of peaceful
demonstrations, strikes and protests that
are far removed from indiscriminate attacks,
the killing of innocent people with the argu-
ment of killing non-believers.

The rejection of German or other foreign pol-
icy must be organized through civilian,
peaceful methods of resistance.

[In Germany there] is real freedom of religion
which does not exist in many Muslim states.
The things that educated people and
preachers can say there cannot be said in
some Muslim countries...There is no prohibi-
tion on the peaceful promotion of Islam.

Many online violent-extremist forum participants rejected El Fazazi's letter on one of two
grounds: either the Moroccan government had tortured him into recanting or El Fazazi
independently veered from the "straight path" of
violent extremism.

Furthermore, El Fazazi's open support for
the German government may undermine his veneer of independence in the letter and may
diminish some of the letter's impact among those
susceptible to violent extremism.

However, El Fazazi includes two arguments that may override some of these personal criticisms. First, he introduces the religious concept of the contract of security and its holy binding nature with regard to immigrants and the state. Second, he factually states that Germany allows greater religious freedom for Muslims than even some Muslim-majority states permit. These two points have the potential to put violent extremists on the defensive and dissuade would-be extremists, especially those in Diaspora communities in Europe.

Nonetheless, unless his letter is translated and marketed beyond the German press, El Fazazi's message will be muted to most Muslim communities opposed to extremism, unengaged with extremism, or at-risk to extremist influences.

Deobandis

Historically, the Deobandis were the religious mentors of the Taliban and many al-Qa`ida adherents. To this day, there are media reports that members and supporters of the Taliban have ties with some of the leading scholars of the Deobandi school of thought.

With these reported extremist ties and veneer of independence (having helped inspire the Taliban's inception and ideology), members of Jamiat Ulama-i-Hind, the leading body of clerics of the Deobandi school of jurisprudential thought, held a conference in November 2009 in Deoband, India in which terrorism was condemned. The conference focused on opposing terrorism, communal strife, disassociating terrorism with Islam, as well as other political issues. Reportedly, tens of thousands attended, including some members of the Darul Uloom. The Darul Uloom is a school that once helped to inspire some Taliban members but subsequently renounced terrorism in a well-publicized February 2008 fatwa.[lx]

Some reporters described the conference as a reiteration of the November 2008 Jamiat Ulama-i-Hind conference and Darul Uloom's 2008 fatwa with regard to counterterrorism statements, with an added expanded agenda concerning political and nationalist issues.

The conference declarations are competing narratives to Taliban and al-Qa`ida propaganda. Strengthening the statements are the presence and tacit approval of tens of thousands of Muslim followers and members of Darul Uloom.

However, Indian government participation at the conference (a minister spoke at the event) and Indian media analysis that characterized the conference as a political event between the government and Jamiat Ulama-i-Hind will likely dampen the conference's potential effects.

The Darul Uloom's counter-violence statements, highlighted and reiterated at the November 2009 conference, still have some potential to put violent extremist ideologues and leaders on the defensive:

> *Islam is a religion of peace and harmony. In Islam, creating social discord or disorder, breach of peace, rioting, bloodshed, pillage or plunder and killing of innocent persons anywhere in the world are all considered most inhuman crimes.*

The Quran clearly states that the killing of even one innocent person is equivalent to massacre of all humankind because it's like opening the floodgates that creates a situation beyond anyone's control; while saving one life is equivalent to the rescue of all humankind.

The extent of Islam's emphasis on peace can be seen from the fact that even while granting the right of self-defense to the oppressed, it insists that no excess be committed in retribution and strictly forbids the targeting of any innocent person.

It is evident from the clear guidelines given in the Holy Quran that the allegation of terrorism against a religion like Islam, which enjoins world peace, is nothing but a lie. In fact, Islam was born to wipe out all kinds of terrorism and to spread the message of global peace.

However, like al-Awdah and El Fazazi, the Deobandi statement suffers from a lack of marketing. While al-Qa`ida messages are translated and broadcast in tiny digestible sound bites, the Deobandi statement is stuck on a couple of websites.

Yemeni Scholars Association

The Yemeni Scholars Association, following media reports of al-Qa`ida in the Arabian Peninsula having directed the failed bombing of an airliner near

Detroit on 25 December 2009, reportedly held consultations with over 150 scholars throughout Yemen to publish a statement on international intervention into Yemeni affairs. Within the statement lies an emotive and simultaneously anti-Western counter violent extremist narrative.

The statement, released during a conference in Sanaʿa on 14 January 2010, includes the following stances.[lxi]

- Yemenis have an obligation to violently oppose foreign forces in Yemen.

- Outside powers must respect Yemen's "sovereignty" and "independence."

- Foreign powers must prevent "meddling" in national affairs or "imposing tutelage" on Yemenis.

- The U.S. President's assurance of no foreign forces in Yemen is valued.

- This policy of non-intervention must be upheld consistently.

- Killing innocent and peaceful people (by anyone) is unlawful.

- Any act of killing outside religious law is non-permissible.

The statement is directed at the United States, the United Kingdom, and any government that some Yemenis feared might intervene against al-Qa`ida in Yemen in the aftermath of the failed 2009 Christmas day bombing over U.S. soil. However, the statement may also be used as is written as a competing narrative against al-Qa`ida.

First, the statement directly objects to killing innocents. In the context of past al-Qa`ida attacks and planned attacks in Yemen and abroad, which either targeted civilians or would have inevitably caused civilian deaths, the press release defies al-Qa`ida ideology. Examples of al-Qa`ida in Yemen attacks targeting civilians were a December 2009 planned attack against a school, the March 2009 assassination of Korean civilians in Yemen, and the failed December 2009 attack against the airliner landing in Detroit.

Second, the statement clearly objects to meddling from outside forces. Although al-Qa`ida in the Arabian Peninsula comprises Yemenis, the organization also includes foreigners and by definition is affiliated with and takes directions from al-Qa`ida core likely based in Pakistan. Therefore, the same words used to "warn" governments about meddling also undercut the legitimacy of al-Qa`ida's influence in Yemen and could resonate with what some analysts describe as Yemen's innate xenophobia in certain provinces.

Third, the statement maintains a nationalist tone, which is inherently critical of al-Qa`ida intentions to not only meddle in Yemen but also to build an international alliance against secular governments in the Middle East and worldwide.

But again, like the messages from other religious leaders, this message has failed to reach international audiences since it has remained untranslated and un-marketed.

The Muslim Council of Denmark

The Muslim Council of Denmark is an umbrella organization claiming to represent dozens of different Muslim groups—over 50,000 Muslims.

In reaction to the 27 October 2009 arrests of a U.S. and a Canadian citizen on charges of conspiracy to commit terrorist acts in Denmark, the Muslim Council of Denmark announced that terrorism is "incompatible with Islam." The Council published the following statements:[lxii]

> *Any act of terrorism is and will always be incompatible with Islam.*
>
> *An attack on any target is the same as an attack on an entire society and its people. We are therefore relieved that the imminent terrorist attacks seem to have been averted.*
>
> *The [Muslim Council of Denmark] stresses that an act of this type would be directly against Islam's basic principles and core values.*

Although few would be likely to view the Muslim Council of Denmark as an authoritative or independent religious source because of its generally constructive relationship with the Danish government, the message may still resound with some would-be violent extremists. The statement may be considered a "consensus" of a Muslim polity of 50,000. Consensus is often a vital legal and moral grounding to help inform pious Muslims to make decisions.

However, because the message was not marketed, it is impossible to know what effect even a message from this somewhat questionably independent source might have on Muslim communities not already part of the Council.

Mardin Artuklu University

On 27–28 March 2010, Turkey's Mardin Artuklu University gathered 15 scholars from around the world to discuss Taqi al-Din Ibn Taymiyya's 14th-century book "Mardin Fatwa," which violent extremists circles often use to justify attacks. Muslim educational non-government organizations Global Center for Renewal and Guidance and Canopus Consulting sponsored the event. The British and Turkish governments also gave financial support. The event aired on al-Jazira television.[lxiii]

The Global Center for Renewal is led by Mauritanian scholar and Saudi Arabia's King Abdul Aziz University teacher Abdullah bin Bayyah and the U.S. head of California's Zaytuna Institute for Islamic Studies. Conference participants offered the following narratives, which were not officially dubbed religious edicts or fatwas:

- Muslim individuals or groups do not have the right to decide on their own to declare or execute violent extremist acts.

- The emergence of governments who protect religious freedoms make the yesteryear divisions between "abodes of Islam" and "abodes of war" invalid.

- Taymiyya's texts to justify violence have been misused because of changed social and political context.

- Taymiyya's texts to justify violence have been misinterpreted out of ignorance about religion.

Critics of the conference, including Turkey's Directorate of Religious Affairs President Ali Bardakoglu and the Turkish media, have made the following statements likely to attempt to undermine the legitimacy of the conference:

- An exercise to invalidate a centuries-old religious view is meaningless.

- The circumstances during Taymiyya's age were similar to today's. Therefore the texts are still applicable.

- The conference is a U.S. and/or UK effort to undermine the Islamic World writ large.

- The British government, in actuality, organized the conference.

- The conference's conclusions do not invalidate earlier fatwas but only allow Muslims to choose between religious judgments.

- The conference's conclusions wrongly rule out justified resistance in the face of unjust oppression such as against the Palestinian occupation.

As explained earlier, Taymiyya attempted to legitimize Muslims killing other Muslims by declaring the target Muslims religiously illegitimate. He lived within the Mamluk state and made this claim so that the Arab Muslim state and individuals would fight the Mongols who occupied Mardin, even though the Mongols claimed to be converted Muslims.

Taymiyya's texts helped inform and inspire twentieth century violent extremist ideologues such as Sayyid Qutb, Abd-al-Salam Faraj, Dr. Fadl, Ayman al-Zawahiri, and Usama bin Ladin, among others.

This conference is an example of substantively well-reasoned and religiously based narratives likely failing to persuade due to assumptions of Western involvement. Even rumors—no matter how baseless—of U.S. or UK influence on the conference are likely to undermine the power the conference's conclusions may have had to inoculate populations against violent extremist propaganda and dissuade those susceptible to radicalization.

Evidence of a lack of impact is that al-Qa`ida and affiliates have mounted very little verbal or textual attack on the findings and conclusions of the conference—al-Qa`ida does not appear to feel threatened. One Iraqi militant group publicly commented on the event, but this was the exception. There was no strong reaction from most violent extremist groups.

Also, the lack of former militant credentials among the hosts and lack of nuanced views of jihad may prevent the conference's conclusions from affecting some would-be extremists and fail to force hardened militants onto the ideological defensive. The event appeared to argue that all violent insurrection is irreligious—a far cry from the beliefs of even peaceful mainstream Muslims who often believe there may be circumstances that warrant politically sanctioned war.

The failings of the conference may offer lessons for more effective competing narrative campaigns. Effective campaigns should amplify, without overt Western involvement, the voices of leaders, theologians, and ideologues who may have former militant experience or more nuanced views of violent insurrection. Bottom line: the messengers of a competing narrative should wield independence and credentials in the eyes of most Muslim communities for a chance at affecting audiences.

Dr. Tahir-ul-Qadri

Popular Pakistani scholar Dr. Tahir-ul-Qadri declared a 2010 600-page Urdu fatwa to renounce suicide bombings and terrorism without any exceptions. He explicitly stated that such acts are forbidden and heretical.

People will listen to Qadri because of his explicit independence from government, constructionist religious views (in some ways resembling Salafi intent to return to only the original Islamic texts to inform modern laws and customs), and education.

Qadri showed his independence when he time and again turned down Pakistani government offers for some of the top religious positions in the region. Among the posts Qadri publicly rejected were Senator for the Upper House of Parliament, Federal Minister for Religious Affairs, Federal Minister for Education, Federal Minister for Law and Parliamentary Affairs, an Ambassadorship, Justice of the Appellate Shari`a Bench for Pakistan's Supreme Court, and Islamic Ideology Council of Pakistan membership. However, somewhat dampening this veneer of independence is Qadri's resume from the early 1980s when he was a Jurist Consult on Islamic law for the Supreme Court and advisor on Islamic curricula for the Federal Ministry of Education. Nonetheless, his more recent professed independence, especially in light of publicly rejecting offers for some of the top Pakistani posts, appears to outweigh these advisory positions in his early career. Qadri appears to be an independent scholar today.

On his website's biography and hammered into his literally thousands of published texts are his constructionist religious views, which would be attractive to many conservative Muslims. He has written that his personal life mission includes "propagation of the true identity of Islamic faith" through "reviving the Prophetic version of Islamic and Quranic teachings..." Qadri expresses goals similar to al-Qa`ida's with regard to actively returning to the "true" teachings of the Prophet. However, Qadri takes the nonviolent and religiously sound route. His messages have the potential to dissuade would-be al-Qa`ida recruits among Muslims from conservative schools of thought.

His credentials as a scholar also may help his fatwa gain some traction with Muslim communities. He studied Islamic studies at the Punjab University in Pakistan and received advanced degrees in law, making him qualified to speak about religious law. This marriage of the theoretical (Islamic studies) and practical (law) makes Qadri an especially dynamic theorist.

Qadri also attained a following in the 1980s with the T.V. show "Understanding the Quran." Today, his satellite show "Speeches of Dr. Tahir-ul-Qadri" offers interpretations and practical applications of Hadith and the Quran using colloquial language. This use of simple, easy-to-understand language is a method al-Qa`ida also uses to reach young people, uneducated persons, or those not already steeped in religious studies. His popular show gives Qadri an audience today that can grow.

His most recent fatwa has the potential to be an effective counter narrative because it is emotive, independent, categorical in its condemnation, empathetic to populist Islamist concerns, and comprehensive.

Emotive - Qadri directly compares violent extremists to Islamic history's greatest extremist villains and killers of the fourth Caliph according to Sunni tradition—the Kharijites:

> *By undertaking a comprehensive analysis of the signs, beliefs and ideologies of the Khawarij through the Qur'anic verses, Prophetic*

> *traditions and jurisprudential opinions of ju-*
> *rists, we have established that the terrorists*
> *are the Khawarij of contemporary times.*[lxiv]

Independent - Qadri states openly his independence from government influence or advice directly in his fatwa's introduction. He appears well aware that rumors of government collusion could undermine his words:

> *We neither seek the pleasure of any gov-*
> *ernment, nor tribute or appreciation from any*
> *international power or organisation. As al-*
> *ways, we have taken the initiative to*
> *perform this task as a part of our religious*
> *obligation.*

Categorical - Qadri leaves little room for interpretation in his damnation of terrorist tactics:

> *These days, the terrorists, in a vain attempt*
> *to impose their own ideas and beliefs and*
> *eliminate their opponents from the face of*
> *the earth, killing innocent people ruthlessly*
> *and indiscriminately everywhere in*
> *mosques, bazaars, governmental offices and*
> *other public places are in fact committing*
> *clear infidelity. They are warned of humiliat-*
> *ing torment in this world and in the*
> *hereafter. Terrorism, in its very essence, is*
> *an act that symbolizes infidelity and rejec-*
> *tion of what Islam stands for. When the*
> *forbidden element of suicide is added to it,*
> *its severity and gravity becomes even*
> *greater.*

Empathetic to populist Islamist concerns – The fatwa condemns terrorism but still acknowledges injustice in Muslim communities:

> *It may be true that among the fundamental local, national and international factors underpinning terrorism on a global level include: the injustices being currently meted out to the Muslims in certain matters, the apparent double standards displayed by the main powers, and their open-ended and long-term military engagements in a number of countries under the pretext of eliminating terror. But the terrorists' recourse to violent and indiscriminate killings have become a routine affair, taking the form of suicide bombings against innocent and peaceful people, bomb blasts on mosques, shrines, educational institutions, bazaars, governmental buildings, trade centres, markets, security installations, and other public places: heinous, anti-human and barbarous acts in their very essence. These people justify their actions of human destruction and mass killing of innocent people in the name of Jihad (holy struggle against evil) and thus distort, twist and confuse the entire Islamic concept of Jihad. This situation is causing Muslims, the young in particular, to fall prey to doubts and reservations, muddling their minds in respect of Jihad, because those perpetrating these atrocities are from amongst the Muslims.*

Comprehensive - The fatwa draws on 172 sources

to include texts from all four major schools of law in Islam:

> *Scores of Qur'anic verses and Prophetic traditions have proved that the massacre of Muslims and terrorism is unlawful in Islam; rather, they are blasphemous acts. This has always been the opinion unanimously held by all the scholars that have passed in the 1400 years of Islamic history, including all the eminent Imams of Tafseer and Hadith and authorities on logic and jurisprudence. Islam has kept the door of negotiation and discussion open to convince by reasoning, instead of the taking up of arms to declare the standpoint of others as wrong, and enforcing one's own opinion. Only the victims of ignorance, jealousy and malice go for militancy. Islam declares them rebels. They will abide in Hell.*
>
> *The conditions leading to the forbiddance of rebellion in the light of the Qur'anic verses, Prophetic traditions and expositions of the jurists are evident. Referring to the holy Companions, their successors, Imam Abu Hanifa, Imam Malik, Imam Shafi'i, Imam Ahmad Bin Hanbal and other leading jurists, the fact has been brought to light that absolute consensus exists among all the leading jurists on the total forbiddance of rebellion against the Muslim state, and there is no difference of opinion between any schools of thought.*

In summary, Qadri's nonprofit states:

> *The comprehensiveness and extent of the original work is meant to leave no doubt, and leave no stone unturned, in order to remove any possible justification for the suicide attacks that the perpetrators or their supporters may offer. Indeed, Dr Tahir-ul-Qadri goes that crucial step forward and announces categorically that suicide bombings and attacks against civilian targets are not only condemned by Islam, but render the perpetrators totally out of the fold of Islam, in other words, to be unbelievers. Furthermore, in what is unprecedented in recent Islamic scholarship, this work draws out scriptural, historical, and classical scholarly references highlighting the obligations of Governments of Islamic nations to deal decisively to root out terrorist elements from society.*

However, it is likely that Qadri's message may have limited impact among those who are outside his South Asian Sufi Barelvi school of thought (with many followers in the United Kingdom, India, and Pakistan). Specifically, Deobandis, who practice a competing conservative school of thought and who helped to inspire the Taliban, may be distrustful of Qadri's message.

Also, much like the other counter-al-Qa`ida narratives in this chapter, Qadri's thick, in-depth 600-page treatise has not reached a global audience as al-Qa`ida's messages have. The story of the fatwa ran in online and print newspapers in Southwest Asia but never became part of a targeted counter-messaging campaign, and never came close to competing with al-Qa`ida's online presence. And Youtube's eight-part series on the edict's release is a far cry from al-Qa`ida's better advertised, pithy, and evocative propaganda videos.[lxv]

FORMER VIOLENT EXTREMISTS

Those who used to execute or promote violence in the name of religion, who now appear to modify their views on violence, often wield the required populist respect and independence from government influence to persuade other Muslims to condemn al-Qa`ida violence.

These authors provide novel arguments that challenge al-Qa`ida's tired reuse of theories that date back decades. New voices point out al-Qa`ida's strategic failure to defeat the West and govern and its willingness to wantonly kill Muslims and foment religious misunderstandings. Al-Qa`ida continues to invent new hooks in an attempt to persuade new audiences, such as Zawahiri's 2007 statement feigning empathy with African-American discrimination in the United States. However, al-Qa`ida's core ideology of violence to defend Islam against Western aggressors remains the same. Former-extremist messages have the potential to break this pattern and the potential to be fresh and newsworthy.

Dr. Fadl

Recanted former extremist ideologue Sayyid Imam al-Sharif (a.k.a. Dr. Fadl) published his third book against al-Qaʿida ideology in January 2010 from his prison in Egypt. *The Future of Conflict in Afghanistan*, published serially in the daily Arabic newspaper al-Sharq al-Awsat, is a disjointed text on Afghanistan, Pakistan, the United States, the Taliban, and al-Qaʿida leadership and history. The text makes the following points on both al-Qaʿida and the United States.

- Al-Qaʿida leaders seek only glory for themselves.

- Al-Qaʿida kills Muslims and has displaced "millions."

- Al-Qaʿida's top leadership holds the primary responsibility for the deaths of Iraqis and Afghans.

- Usama bin Ladin exploits distrust of the United States to justify murder.

- Al-Qaʿida can claim no tangible successes. (Dr. Fadl moves away from religious to pragmatic argumentation with this point.)

- There is a chasm between al-Qaʿida's goals and capability: al-Qaʿida cannot reach its ends through its current violent means.

- A U.S. surge in Afghanistan will lead to more recruitment for al-Qa'ida and more Afghani deaths.

- The United States lacks values (such criticism likely gives Fadl a veneer of independence).

His previous books, which also highlight al-Qa'ida leadership impiety and narcissism, were published in 2007 and 2008.[lxvi]

Fadl's preeminent credentials as a former extremist leader, fighter, ideologue, and author, along with religion- and humanity-based arguments help to make his texts potentially persuasive.

Up until fall of 2007, Fadl was internationally renowned for penning the al-Qa'ida playbook *Foundations of the Preparations for Jihad* on top of a body of literature providing theological guidance and tactical lessons for violent extremists worldwide. U.S. Military Academy's Combating Terrorism Center assesses that ideologically Fadl's earlier texts are still as influential as Usama bin Ladin's words.

Following his 2003 arrest in Yemen and subsequent extradition to Egypt, Fadl worked on his first book, declaring that the ends do not justify the means in violent extremism. In this first text, he vilifies al-Qa'ida tactics of killing innocents, stealing money, and wantonly using Muslims as human shields. Because the manuscript also condemns secularism and the West, he may continue to earn a fair readership among would-be al-Qa'ida sympathizers distrustful of

Western intentions. Along with his second and third publications, this first text is timeless.

The following are quotations from his first book:

> *There is no such thing in Islam as ends justifying the means.*
>
> *If vice becomes mixed with virtue, all becomes sinful.*
>
> *There is nothing that invokes the anger of God and His wrath like the unwarranted spilling of blood and wrecking property.*
>
> *On the day of judgment every double crosser will have a banner up his anus proportional to his treachery.*
>
> *Oh, you young people, do not be deceived by the heroes of the internet, the leaders of the microphones, who are launching statements inciting youth while living...in a distant cave...they have thrown many others before you into the infernos, graves, and prisons.*
>
> *Those who have triggered clashes and pressed their brothers into unequal military confrontations are specialists neither in fatwas nor in military affairs.*[lxvii]

Ayman al-Zawahiri suggested in a summer 2007 audio message that torture drove Fadl's renunciation, in an attempt to undermine the impact of the first book prior to its publication. However, Fadl, in a 2007 interview, explicitly compared his authorship inside prison with Taymiyya. Taymiyya was a medieval ideologue, whom many violent extremists revere and cite for justification of violence and who wrote his seminal texts independently in prison. Fadl appeared to out-argue Zawahiri's point in this case.

Furthermore, Fadl's texts have not led to his release from prison, further suggesting that he wrote the book out of free will without personal agenda.

In 2008, Zawahiri even wrote a 188-page defense against Fadl's accusations, which

- Gave Dr. Fadl further legitimacy and publicity.

- Squandered al-Qa`ida leadership time.

- Revealed al-Qa`ida's fear of the effect of counter-violence messages.

- Forced Zawahiri to restate his justifications for violent attacks that kill civilians.

All three texts, along with Fadl's interviews since 2007, still have the potential to resound more strongly with a worldwide audience. Fadl's arguments that rest on humanity, piety, and common sense are universal and timeless themes.

However, Fadl's texts remain largely un-translated and un-marketed when compared to al-Qa`ida leadership messages, which a worldwide network of independent marketers and translators buttress. As long as Fadl's texts remain in Arabic in Arabic newspapers, the books' serialized chapters will not de-legitimize or undermine al-Qa`ida's ability to persuade.

Gama`a Islamiyya

In the late 1980s, Gama`a Islamiyya (GI), an extremist offshoot of the Muslim Brotherhood, amassed funds from different local mosque-centered groups to fight the government and any entity that GI felt "un-Islamic" from their peculiar perspective. In the 1990s, GI conducted a concerted campaign of violent extremism targeting tourists, foreigners, state officials, intellectuals, and rivals. From 1992–1997, GI reportedly killed over 1,200, including a counterterrorism police chief, a parliamentary speaker, and dozens of innocent bystander "collateral damage." In 1997, with tens of thousands of affiliates, supporters, and militants imprisoned, GI announced its unconditional renunciation of violence and the halt of all violent acts against the state. GI published 15 books on its recantation while in prison.

After nearly a decade of GI's books remaining largely un-translated, unpublished, and un-marketed, GI began publishing its competing narratives online. The website and its "English" counterpart (egyig.com/en/) comprise essays and statements on current affairs, Islamic issues, and counterterrorism treatises.

Essays on phenomena of violence and religion include "Jihad and Misunderstanding," "To Whom Jihad is Directed?," "Distinction Between Combatants and Civilians," and "Types of Jihad."

The following are quotations taken from GI essays on violent extremist attacks:

> *...Islam today witnesses several acts of jihad, some of which represent examples of sacrifice while the rest break Islamic law— whether out of good intentions or ignorance.*

> *Jihad is like other Islamic duties and judgments—necessary or prohibited according to the rules on the implementation of jihad.*

> *...women, children, priests, the elderly, farmers, workers, and peaceful persons...these people are whom we call civilians. Scholars forbid fighting these people...This is a ban by the Prophet Himself.*

> *All these groups of people should [however] be killed if they fight Muslims or aid the enemies of Muslims.*

> *Islam refuses to follow barbarism, which allows killing children...*

> *Jihad has morals.*

> *Islam respects humanity and never intends to kill people without reasons.*

> *Defensive jihad is obligatory, but jihad for religious promotion outside of Muslim borders is optional...Jihad for promoting Islam is not found in Islamic law.*

*Those who misunderstand the concept of ji-
had and conduct terrorist attacks do not only
kill innocents and illegally steal money, but
they also turn others against [lawful] jihad.*

*Those people fight only to call themselves
warriors. They have no goals...They do not
think of the ramifications of their actions.
Moreover, they misinterpret the laws of jihad
so much that some allow the killing of
women and children, killing other innocent
persons, killing for nationality, and refusing
to make peace with enemies...Such wrong
actions are against our religion—[and cause]
some to accuse Islam for being unmerciful
and unforgiving...*[lxviii]

The renunciations have the potential to affect those who are susceptible to radicalization
today because of their sound grounding in accepted Islamic concepts of laws of war and
emphasis on piety and humanity, especially with
regard to the prohibition of killing innocents. Furthermore the statements are nuanced—allowing
for some kinds of violence such as state-
sanctioned defense against oppression. But, according to GI, al-Qa`ida's ideology allowing
indiscriminate killing is never permitted under
any circumstances.

However, the English translations on the
GI website are riddled with grammatical and spell-
ing errors to the point at which the language is
unprofessional and at times incomprehensible to
English readers (I translated these particular excerpts and could not rely on GI's poor translation

attempts). This weak translation, likely a result of free online translation software or untrained translators, highlights the difficulty and importance of accurate, professional, and engaging translation to deliver a message.

Also, the messages lay immobile on the website, with a low ranking even in Egypt, and with no observable attempt to market to Muslim communities worldwide. The website has a relatively low and un-diverse viewership. It is ranked 5,253 in viewership in Egypt, with 51 other sites displaying links to egyig.com/en/. Almost 100 percent of visitors found the site through Google. Almost half of the viewers are located in Egypt, 23.2 percent in Saudi Arabia, 6.3 percent in Algeria, 3.8 percent in Morocco, and 2.7 percent in the U.A.E.[lxix]

Libyan Islamic Fighting Group

The imprisoned leadership of the Libyan Islamic Fighting Group (LIFG), a group that was previously a devoted and official al-Qa`ida affiliate, published in September 2009 an Arabic-language refutation of over 400 pages detailing contentious aspects of al-Qa`ida's violent ideology. Rumors abound in the Arab world that GI's texts were used as an anonymous source for this recantation.

The manuscript includes the following translated quotations, which could be effective in a counter-al-Qa`ida marketing campaign. The quotations were translated by Mohammed Ali Musawi and published by the Quilliam Foundation:

The reduction of jihad to fighting with the sword is an error and shortcoming.

It is impermissible to leave for jihad without the permission of parents and lenders.

There are ethics and morals to jihad—among which are: that the jihad is for the sake of God, and the illegality of killing women, children, the elderly...

Also among the ethics and morals in jihad is the proscription of treachery, the obligation to keep promises, the obligation of kindness to prisoners of war, the impermissibility of the mutilation of the dead...

The opinion of those that follow the traditions of Muhammad has settled upon the impermissibility of resorting to arms to change political situations.

Fighting because of sectarianism, tribalism, or social position and fighting for worldly matter or power fall under the category of forbidden civil war.

The legitimate alternatives to using violence for reform and change are enjoining good and forbidding evil and da'wah.

The historical examples which the people of the Prophet's tradition have agreed upon: the impermissibility of fighting rulers and governors, and their agreement that patience and

*calling to God and enjoining good and for-
bidding evil is the correct way.*

*Some of the reasons for extremism are the
prevalence of sins in Muslim societies, an
absence of a correct understanding of religion and reality, emotional reactions,
unqualified people taking the lead and the
absence of comprehensive education among
others.*

The text includes a statement that violence
is only obligatory in certain places at certain
times, such as when non-believers invade Muslim
countries. War is permissible for residents and
neighbors of the invaded region, such as Palestinian territories, Iraq, and Afghanistan.

Though a seemingly subtle point, this argument undermines the extremist narrative core
al-Qa`ida figures like Ayman al-Zawahiri and Abu
Yahya al-Libi propagate. These individuals com-
monly argue that jihad is a duty incumbent upon
all able-bodied Muslims (*fard 'ayn*) without exception, at all times. Despite this nuance, LIFG still
condemns the very pillars of al-Qa`ida.

Despite public assumptions of Libyan government coercion, the text still has the potential to
dissuade some would-be violent extremists worldwide. LIFG has the ideological weight, street
credibility, and personal networks to deliver a
counter-violence narrative that may resonate with
Muslims susceptible to al-Qa`ida messaging.

However, compared with Dr. Fadl's
counter-violence literature and Gama'a Islamiyya's
1990s recantations of terrorism, the LIFG text

more stringently emphasizes the impermissibility of attacking a secular state government. This gives the appearance of some appeasement to the Libyan government and may indicate some direct Libyan government intervention with the substance of the text.

Nonetheless, the text also shows integrity with its anti-invader bent. Compared with previous terrorism renunciations, this statement more clearly and directly supports violent attacks against invading forces and specifically supports insurgency operations and terrorist attacks in Iraq, Afghanistan, and Israel. The overt anti-Western and anti-Israeli sentiment in the statement will likely bolster the statement's impact among those with a propensity to violent extremism who are also distrustful of the West and Israel.

But like the other sources discussed in this book, the long manuscript, as is, will unlikely compete with al-Qa`ida messaging. First, the format requires the target audience to be literate and have access to the Internet and newspapers through which it was distributed. Second, this recantation is verbose, while al-Qa`ida's narrative is streamlined into locally attractive sound bites available in multiple languages on multiple media platforms. Therefore, while this document highlights—with nuance—exploitable vulnerabilities in al-Qa`ida's ideology, to sufficiently compete for the attention of those susceptible to supporting or joining al-Qa`ida, the LIFG recantation should be marketed through independent and non-Western media outlets and integrated sound bites and images on counter-extremist websites, videos, text messages, pamphlets, and disks.

Nasir Abas

Nasir Abas was a leader of Indonesia's *Jama`a Islamiyya* but left the group when it began to attack civilians and partner with al-Qa`ida elements and sympathizers. Abas has since written a book and conducted numerous interviews about his disgust over violence against civilians in the name of religion.

The following are his quotes during a 2005 interview:

> *Our job is just to protect our belief in Islam, to protect the Muslims, to protect our homeland. That is jihad. But if you—if we are—if jihad is meaning to kill the civilians, non-Muslim, that is not jihad.*

> *...because what I'm teaching [jihad] is just for use for in battlefield, to use for defending their homeland.*

> *I feel upset when I heard some of my friends, some of my students, some of my relatives, you know, like Ali Grufanis, he is my brother-in-law. He is involved in the Bali bombs of October. So I feel upset, yeah. I think that this is the wrong way they have chosen. They misused the knowledge.*

*...this is a chance and the time for me to ex-
plain to the people, you know, that the
ideology is wrong.*

*We explain to them that the ideology is devi-
ant, it's deviation of Islam, a
misunderstanding, misinterpretation about—
Islam is about the holy Koran.*

Although Abas' messages are a few years
old, they are still viable counter narratives as they
rely on universal pious and humanitarian arguments and could still be persuasive. But like the
LIFG renunciation, rumor of government collaboration will likely hinder Abas' words from affecting
all audiences. Furthermore, like the LIFG recantation, Abas' renunciation is nuanced, explaining
that some forms of violence are permissible but al-
Qa'ida's violent ideology is unacceptable.

Hassan Hattab

Hassan Hattab, founder of Algeria's Salafist Group
for Preaching and Combat, quit in 2003 after a
supposed dispute concerning the legitimacy of
targeting civilians. Hattab reportedly surrendered
to Algerian authorities in late September 2007 and
since then has made several calls for extremists to
lay down arms.

Hattab, in articles circulated in the Algerian press, has drawn on religious texts and
morality to condemn terrorist attacks in Algeria.
The Algerian government has used Hattab's
statements as a cornerstone of its information operations in an attempt to prevent radicalization

and promote rehabilitation, de-radicalization, and disengagement:[lxx]

> *Al-Qa`ida is killing and shedding the blood of Muslims by planting bombs without differentiating between children and adults, or between men and women, under the pretext of targeting the regime.*

> *This includes the mass killing of children, women, and old people by explosions. The group also are kidnapping, frightening, extorting, and threatening people to get money in order to continue the jihad, they claim.*

> *What law or moral code could allow this?*

> *Is this really a jihad that would please God?*

> *[Acts of terrorism] do nothing for Islam or Muslims and against which I have already given warnings in the past.*

> *Return [violent extremists] to society and your families; society is ready to welcome you and heal the wounds.*

Such a statement from a former anti-government leader known for his devotion to Islam and his former ferocity could play well to Muslim communities outside of the Algerian press' limited audience, even though Hattab's messages will likely always be partially anchored to criticisms that the Algerian government propaganda exploits his words.

Syed Hashmi

Pakistani-born U.S. citizen Syed Hashmi—charged for sheltering and aiding a known al-Qa`ida militant in London between 2004 and 2006—made a startling 20-minute court statement, which included counterterrorism narratives.

He stated:

> *I did it when I was ignorant of Allah and his message.*

> *Muslims cannot wage war against non-Muslims in their host country.*

> *Yes, I was wrong in helping my brothers the noble mujahidin, but they will always be in my prayers.*

He also states that his "many mistakes" were due to his own misunderstandings of religion and claims that the United States mistreated imprisoned Muslims.

His respect for mujahidin and distrust of U.S. intentions may help to make his statements about misunderstanding religion resound with Muslims "on the fence" with regards to supporting (passively or actively) violent extremism. His statement alone will unlikely spark communities to action. But along with the sea of other counter narratives—outlined in this book—it may help to inspire and give ideological ammunition to some community leaders to undercut al-Qa`ida violent ideology.

Nasser al-Bahri

Former Usama bin Ladin bodyguard and self-declared reformed extremist Nasser al-Bahri has the credentials to be an effective voice against al-Qa`ida ideology. His former extremist credentials—why would-be recruits may look up to him and listen to his words—include wide battlefield experience, imprisonment, and his anti-West stance.

He fought in Bosnia, Somalia, Tajikistan, and Afghanistan. His fighting savvy landed him with one of the most trusted positions in al-Qa`ida—personal security guard for al-Qa`ida's top figurehead Usama bin Ladin himself. Compare this with the seeming cowardice of non-veteran talking heads like Anwar al-Awlaki. Clearly Bahri commands respect when he enters a room.

After a supposed personal argument with bin Ladin, Bahri left Afghanistan for Yemen in 2000. There, Yemeni officials imprisoned him for terrorism for 18 months. In prison, as is often the case for violent extremists, he likely became ever closer with terrorist cell leaders and violent ideology. Nonetheless, he renounced terrorism upon release. Imprisonment may add to his extremist mystique, hardened nature, and potential draw for those susceptible to radicalization. Imprisonment gives him "street cred."

His stance on "jihad" is nuanced, adding further to his allure. While some counter-al-Qa`ida voices are completely against violent extremists and may thus turn off ideological fence-sitters, Bahri has a balanced message. He acknowledges "ideological differences with the West" and "injustice" against Muslims. He believes that "jihad" is permissible and takes on many forms—

to include education, which is Bahri's "jihad" of choice. Also, he still shows personal respect for bin Ladin. Asked in an interview what he would do if he were to face al-Qa'ida's leader again, Bahri answered:

> *Actually if I had the chance to meet Sheikh Osama, I would kiss him on his head, his forehead and cheeks. I would ask him to pray for me, because I am engaged in another form of jihad. I am in a battle where I use my own methods to raise awareness among the youth, and build their capacity so that they can lead a normal life.*[lxxi]

His credentials as a former extremist, former prisoner, and nuanced ideologue will likely help Bahri deliver his counter-al-Qa'ida messages.

Themes he repeats are that killing innocents is unacceptable; al-Qa'ida lacks a clear vision; and al-Qa'ida has no legitimacy without religious, legal, or scholarly experts. As Bahri states:

> *I would say that the bombings taking place today in Yemen, which are meant to disrupt public peace as part of a certain agenda of killing innocent people, are unacceptable. The problem of al-Qaeda outside of Afghanistan is that it does not have a clear strategy, and it is not part of an overall hierarchical structure, and it does not have legitimacy as a religious and legal entity, such as working under the leadership of scholars. The fact is that these organizations have two or three students who issue fatwa's, and this is*

> *wrong. That is why I urge young people not to hasten to take up arms and engage in fighting in order to preserve lives, which Allah has forbidden to take except with proper justification. Killing committed out of emotional reactions or anger is not Jihad...* "[lxxii]

TERRORISM VICTIMS

Another pool of potentially convincing credible voices are the victims of violent extremism. Their credentials lie in firsthand accounts of the downside of violent extremism. Their voices are capable of bridging the geographic and temporal gap to inspire hatred against al-Qa`ida within communities that are not actively suffering from al-Qa`ida-inspired attacks.

Victims could include persons who were rescued just prior to being forced to be unwilling suicide bombers, surviving victims of attacks, and families that have lost loved ones in terrorist attacks—either suicide bomber perpetrators coaxed into joining al-Qa`ida or their victims.

The following includes two examples of rescued would-be child suicide bombers. I chose these two examples to illustrate the potential persuasive power of victims because these cases are especially egregious: forcing pre-adolescents to blow themselves up. In most cases, such victims of inhumane exploitation are killed. Many young handicapped and mentally retarded victims were used as unwitting human bomb deliverers in Iraq from 2004–2007. Handlers blew up the unwilling victims before they could be rescued. However, the BBC was able to interview two young survivors in

Pakistan in 2009 and 2010.

Child Victim #1

In November 2009, a 14-year-old boy from north-west Pakistan, now in Pakistani army custody, told his story of being kidnapped, drugged, and forced into being a suicide bomber to a BBC correspondent.[lxxiii]

The boy explained the following:

- Militants came to his village and threatened to behead his father if the boy did not join them.

- The extremists said they would behead the boy if he did not become a suicide bomber.

- The boy was "brainwashed" (his own words) to believe his suicide would lead to heaven.

- The boy was regularly beaten—with scars still on his back during the interview—and went without food for five days at one point.

- He was given "pills" which dulled his senses before a suicide mission.

- The boy refused to ignite his suicide vest in a targeted mosque and then fled back to his family and the police.

This story is one of many reports corroborating that the Taliban and al-Qa`ida recruit, indoctrinate, and employ young children as suicide bombers.

Child fighters are common in Afghanistan. During the Russian invasion in the 1990s, for example, teenagers were considered adults in Afghani and Pakistani communities. However, using the unwilling young as suicide bombers is a tactic that has become apparent only in the past two years in Afghanistan. It is unprecedented.

Unconfirmed press reports suggest al-Qa`ida and the Taliban in Pakistan and Afghanistan use children as young as six as suicide bombers. In some cases, kidnappers sell children for $6,000–$14,000 USD (Pakistan's per-capita income is approximately $2,600 USD per year) depending on how quickly the bomber is needed and how close the child is located to a planned attack. In some cases, children are bartered between Taliban or al-Qa`ida cells.

In October 2008 in South Waziristan, the Pakistani government uncovered a Taliban-run and al-Qa`ida-associated training camp for pre-adolescent suicide bombers. Pakistani security forces described the training camp as a "nursery" or "factory" for suicide bombers.

In July 2009, Pakistani soldiers claimed to have saved "dozens" of would-be pre-adolescent suicide bombers and stated that there may have been as many as 300–400 such children still in captivity elsewhere at that time.

Although the Pakistani military claims to attempt to "rehabilitate" rescued children at schools run by the army on army bases, there is no independent probe to study the potential success of such de-radicalization, rehabilitation, or reintegration courses.

Thus far, news stories rarely focus on specific and emotive cases of child exploitation. Instead, general stories of coerced and kidnapped children have usually made headlines modestly in Pakistan and the West. These non-specific reports have appeared to do little to dissuade the Taliban and al-Qa`ida from using young people as suicide bombers or to turn Pakistanis and Afghans viscerally against the Taliban. Even a January 2009 UN statement acknowledging and condemning the use of child suicide bombers has failed to act as a viable competing narrative.

This case of the would-be 14-year-old suicide bomber, if this voice is amplified (on Youtube with subtitles in dozens of languages, for example), has the potential to inspire citizenry towards more active vigilance and action against violent extremism. This rare occasion of a child speaking openly to the press provides a personal perspective previously unseen. His words have the potential to cause popular visceral disgust over this al-Qa`ida strategy employed by al-Qa`ida affiliates and partners throughout the world.

The 14-year-old's quotes can be an emotional competing narrative that undermines Taliban and al-Qa`ida claims of piety and morals. In the boy's words:

> *[The Taliban] said: 'You have two choices. We will behead you, or you will become a suicide bomber.' I refused.*

If we refused they would tie our hands be-hind our backs, blindfold us and start beating us.

They brainwashed us and told us we would go to heaven.

We used to ask [the Taliban] to let us out to pray. They would reply 'you are already on your way to heaven. You don't need to pray.'

They beat me hard for five days. I wasn't given any food.

Before the mission they took me to a dark room and started giving me pills.

Before the Taliban came we used to enjoy freedom. We used to play, and go to our schools.

The Taliban had beaten me so harshly my back was scarred. When my parents saw that my mother started to cry...

I want to tell the Taliban that they are cruel, and what they did to me was unjust. I can't kill innocent Muslims.

I am not afraid of [the Taliban]. I am only afraid of God. I am answerable only to Him.

Child Victim #2

A 13-year-old Pakistani girl reportedly fled a Taliban stronghold where her family was forcing her to become a suicide bomber. Under the supervision of the Pakistani police in a "secure" location, she told her account to BBC in a 3-minute video. The following is a summarized account of her story:[lxxiv]

- Her father and brother were pressuring her to carry out a suicide attack—explaining she would go to paradise.

- She argued about all the innocent people she would kill in such an attack.

- Her older brother "Ismail" reportedly previously helped plan other suicide attacks including an October 2009 bombing in Peshawar which killed more than 50 people.

- Her brother also supposedly dispatched her nine-year-old sister "Nahida." In the BBC account, the 13-year-old describes her brother and father attaching a bomb to her sister and connecting strips and wires throughout the nine-year-old's clothing. She said her sister "was crying very loud for [her] mother" when she was taken away. The brother claimed the younger girl carried out a suicide operation in Afghanistan.

- The 13-year-old finished the interview stating the "Taliban should be burned alive."

There is no independent verification of her account. However, Pakistani police officers claim they assess she is telling the truth from her "natural" attitude and pieces of information from her story they can supposedly confirm. They claimed they did not see any indication of exaggeration.

The video, showing her face, tears, and expressions of anger and horror, gives depth and potential emotionality to the story of the Taliban's and al-Qaʾida's child victims. The successful use of a nine-year-old girl as a suicide bomber in the story is especially repugnant and may help to engender mistrust and disgust for violent extremism.

The video is a narrative that, if translated and widely disseminated, has the potential to undermine any veneer of religious legitimacy that the Taliban and al-Qaʾida' enjoy. And any video would be a force multiplier to a competing narrative campaign to counter al-Qaʾida's visual and evocative marketing.

Documentary: Children of the Taliban

Award-winning documentary filmmaker and renowned journalist Sharmeen Obaid-Chinoy has been reporting on the Taliban in Afghanistan and Pakistan since 2001. Her documentary "Children of the Taliban" shows the radicalization of child suicide bombers firsthand through interviews and careful reporting. For example, her film focuses on young men Masood, Sadiq, and Zainulah who individually blew themselves up in Taliban suicide operations killing between 6 and 28 others.

The filmmaker summarizes the recruitment and training process into five stages:

First, Taliban "prey" on the large impoverished rural families who are unable to take care of or educate their children as much as they wish. The Taliban promise the parents that the extremist group will educate, feed, and take care of the children—a promise too often too good to pass up by caring and unwitting parents.

Second, the Taliban teach the children only the Quran in its original classical Arabic—a language these children do not speak, read, or understand. Teachers forbid any other type of information such as newspapers, radio, or books and "severely" punish students found with literary contraband.

Third, the Taliban instructors do all they can to make the child victims hate the material world. During her presentations, Sharmeen claims she has seen instructors physically beat boys. Also, the Taliban only feed dry bread and water to children twice a day, forbid playing games, force children to read the Quran for at least eight hours per day, and prohibit the students from leaving even to see family. Essentially the children are kidnapped prisoners, and the parents do not have the financial or logistical means to rescue them if the family learns of the abusive environment.

Fourth, seasoned Taliban fighters discuss their exploits through romantic stories and videos with the stolen children. The kids are taught of the food, honey, and women that await them at the other side of suicide. Also, the fighters promise that the pupils will be made heroes in the eyes of their families and neighborhoods and that their families will be taken care of financially after their deaths.

Fifth, the Taliban overload the youngsters with high-quality emotive propaganda videos with gruesome images of Muslim victims of Western and secular government attacks in Iraq, Afghanistan, and Pakistan. The Taliban teach their soon-to-be suicide bombers that Western governments and allies and all civilians are fair game in warfare. The children reportedly believe, at the end, that "Islam is under attack" and the only recourse is suicide operations.

As the filmmaker says:

> *They are promised lakes of milk and honey and virgins in the afterlife. The young boys I speak with say to me: Why would I want to live in this world—where they rely on charity, dry pieces of bread and water, where they are subjected to harsh treatment—when they can be free and be the envy of their colleagues in the afterlife. They are only too eager to sign on the dotted line and join the ranks of the Taliban."*

If the full documentary—along with the filmmaker's interviews and presentations—is re-broadcast worldwide with subtitles in dozens of languages, the stories of these child victims have a chance at resounding with Muslims communities yet unaffected by the Taliban and al-Qa`ida.

Death Making

Many victims' stories are shown on Arabic-language satellite television station Al-Arabiya's Sinat al-Mawt (Death Making), a one-hour show exposing terrorism's victims. Interviews include imprisoned violent extremists, families of those who entered violent extremism, and families of attack victims. According to a 2009 University of Maryland opinion poll, 25 percent of Arab respondents claimed they watched al-Arabiya "almost daily."

The show, its host, and its general manager Abdul Rahman al-Rashed have received threats, including a death threat from al-Qa'ida in Iraq and a rebuke from al-Qa'ida second-in-command Ayman al-Zawahiri.[lxxv] These threats, along with continued edgy and bloody reporting, will likely continue to increase viewership.

Nonetheless, the show will likely only attract those already against violent extremism who actively tune in with the purpose of learning even more about al-Qa'ida's violent ideology and trail of victims. And since most Muslims do not speak Arabic—the language of the show—the show is linguistically limited in its reach. Therefore, it is essential that these stories are translated and re-broadcast to reach as wide an audience as possible worldwide, to help dissuade those vulnerable to al-Qa'ida influences and to help leaders and social movements in need of narratives to justify counter-al-Qa'ida activities.

For example, pithy video cuts with subtitles could saturate Youtube and independent websites, targeting a wide audience comprising those that may otherwise not tune in to al-Arabiyya. Bottom line: videos should be available to those not actively looking for the videos in the first place.

13. THE MESSAGE: THE WORDS THAT EXPLOIT AL-QA`IDA'S VULNERABILITY

As explained in the introduction to the previous chapter, one must judge a potentially inspiring message by its source and substance. The last chapter focused on the source; this chapter will focus on the substance.

It is worth analyzing messages thematically because some counter narratives come from sources that do not fit easily into the categories in the previous chapter. Furthermore, a powerful message from a relatively unknown or anonymous source could have some potential to dissuade would-be extremists or bait al-Qa`ida ideologues into defending their positions.

Most importantly though, the last chapter's voices may help to inspire local community leaders to develop their own narratives. And these narratives—at the local level—may have an excellent chance at reaching would-be recruits. Like the previous voices, anyone speaking along the following themes may help to starve al-Qa`ida of future support and recruits.

Wanton Tatarrus

Wanton tatarrus is al-Qa`ida's Achilles' heel. Wanton tatarrus is the gratuitous murder of innocents and is the rubric/excuse al-Qa`ida uses to murder.

According to the Iraq Body Count as of April 2010 (an independent U.S./UK Group), terrorists and religiously driven insurgents were the greatest contributor to the 95,888–104,595 innocent Iraqi civilians who met violent deaths since 2003. The Associated Press had civilian violent deaths at 110,600 as of April 2009. These numbers contrast starkly with the 4,711 coalition deaths in Iraq since 2003. Bottom line: al-Qa`ida primarily kills Muslims.

Al-Qa`ida's defensive reactions, in hundreds of video and audio messages and thousands of pages of text, are evidence of this critical vulnerability. The group's reaction can be categorized as follows:

Vilification - At times, as in Ayman al-Zawahiri's 2005 letter to the late al-Qa`ida Iraq leader Abu Musab Zarwaqai imploring him to curb his killing of Iraqi civilians, al-Qa`ida has come right out and announced this vulnerability. It is a vulnerability that if exposed would curb al-Qa`ida's ability to attract recruits and support.

Admittance & Justification – At other times, as in Abu Yahya al-Libi's 2006 essay "Tatarrus in Modern Jihad," al-Qa`ida tries to justify killing innocents, claiming that the laws from the Prophet Muhammad are in need of modernizing to reflect "modern" guerilla warfare. (Al-Libi is an al-Qa`ida ideologue and leader.)

Denial - And, at other times, al-Qa`ida has outright lied on its confirmed record of wanton tatarrus. For example, al-Qa`ida publishing organization al-Sahab filmed and released Adam Gadahn's (a.k.a. Azzam al-Amriki) 18-minute video "The Mujahidin Do Not Target Muslims" in

December 2009.[lxxvi] Gadahn is a U.S. citizen who is reportedly a media spokesman for al-Qa`ida. In the video (in English with accurate Arabic subtitles), Gadahn claims al-Qa`ida and affiliates are innocent of recent large-scale bombings in Pakistan. He claims governments are behind the attacks, and the media is in collaboration with governments to blame violent extremists. The following are excerpts:

> *These criminal acts usually result in large numbers of casualties, especially among women and children. And invariably, the enemies of Islam and Muslims pin the blame for them on the mujahidin. And invariably, the mujahidin's denials of responsibility fall on deaf ears, whereas the uncorroborated allegations of the regimes are carried without criticism and in a one-sided way by the so-called independent media in Islamabad, Kabul, and other world capitals. Why? Because these media are now willing weapons of propaganda in the pockets of the Crusaders and their puppet governments and armies allied with them.*
>
> *They want us to believe that these same mujahidin are now so at a loss for targets that they have been reduced to bombing innocent Muslims, shopkeepers, shoppers, and commuters, and killing and maiming defenseless men, women, and children without mercy and without regard for morality, principles, and the laws of Allah.*

> *Who are the likelier culprits...are they muja-*
> *hidin...who have dedicated their very lives*
> *to the implementation of Islam and its*
> *shari'a, which forbids the taking of even one*
> *innocent life?*
>
> *But what the puppet media don't tell you is*
> *that the mujahidin have condemned, and*
> *continue to condemn, all attacks which in-*
> *discriminately kill and wound innocent*
> *Muslims in their markets, mosques, streets,*
> *schools, and homes.*
>
> *And we ask Allah...to have mercy on those*
> *killed...We also express the same in regard*
> *to the unintended Muslim victims of the mu-*
> *jahidin's operations against the Crusaders*
> *and their allies and puppets...*

There is overwhelming evidence and independent verification that violent extremist groups
affiliated with al-Qa`ida and its members did in
fact conduct a slew of mass bombings in Pakistan
leading to this particular message of outright denial. And al-Qa`ida leadership likely feels
vulnerable to public backlash over its attacks.

Killing innocents helped to staunch support for violent extremist movements in Egypt and
Algeria in the 1990s and Iraq from 2007 to the
present day. To repeat this trend, effective competing narratives will underline the inhumanity
and impiety of al-Qa`ida targeting innocents in
attacks.

There is already evidence that innocent
victims turn Muslims off to al-Qa`ida. Wide

counter-violence messaging would deepen this effect. Muslims in Africa and Asia have increasingly rejected suicide bombings and violence against civilians from 2002 to 2010.

The downward trend indicates that advocates of suicide attacks are capable of changing their views on a substantial scale in a short time. Statements emphasizing civilian casualties of terrorist attacks would likely encourage further rejection of terrorist tactics.

A June 2010 extensive Pew Study found that support for terrorist tactics declined in six countries from 2002–2010:[lxxvii]

Lebanon:	74 percent → 39 percent
Pakistan:	33 percent → 8 percent
Jordan:	43 percent → 20 percent
Indonesia:	26 percent → 15 percent
Nigeria:	47 percent → 34 percent
Turkey:	13 percent → 6 percent

The study provides a road map for undermining the violent extremist ideology that it is okay to kill innocents in the name of God. Muslims, by a wide margin, do not approve of the tactic, and translated and disseminated messages should further solidify al-Qaʿida's critics and dissuade new recruits and supporters.

In exposing wanton tatarrus, there is evidence that humanizing a victim's story can most effectively help galvanize citizens against violent extremism versus just announcing cold macro-statistics of innocent deaths.

For example, in 1993 the Egyptian government and government-influenced media released the details of the death of a 12-year old schoolgirl who was "collateral damage" in a terrorist attack. The media release influenced citizens against violent extremism.

In November 1993, the EIJ, many members of which would later comprise a core contingent within al-Qa`ida as explained earlier in this book, detonated a car bomb in an attempt to assassinate prime minister Atef Sidqi. The car bomb exploded near a Cairo school for girls. The prime minister was unhurt in his armored car, but the blast injured 21 people and killed one. The only death was young Shayma Abd-al-Halim, who was crushed by a door blown loose in the blast.

The press and Government used her death to rouse hatred against violent extremists in Egypt. The *New York Times* replayed the story for a worldwide audience in 1993:

> *'We were sitting in the English classroom,' said teacher Samih Yunis, his sweater and pants stained with blood. 'We heard an explosion. We all ducked and started to run downstairs. They told me that Shayma Mohammed Abdel Halim was injured. I ran back to get her and carried her out in my arms. She was silent and dying.'*

> *The father of the 11-year-old girl [she was later reported to be 12] came to the school two hours after the attack to take her home. When onlookers told him she had been injured and taken to a hospital, he threw his arms into the air.*

'My daughter!' he cried. 'My daughter! Someone take me to my daughter!' He was helped into a car by several onlookers and whisked away.

According to the press, "Shayma's death captured people's emotions as nothing else had." The media reported that when her coffin was carried through the streets of Cairo, people yelled and chanted, "terrorism is the enemy of God."

In discussing the importance of the event to his group's demise, former EIJ leader Ayman al-Zawahiri wrote, "The government used the death of Shayma, may she rest in peace, and portrayed the incident as an attack by the [EIJ] against Shayma..."

Her story helped strip the EIJ of its sympathizers and provided security forces with greater liberty to operate publicly and more aggressively. Within two years, EIJ leadership, including the current al-Qa`ida top lieutenant Ayman al-Zawahiri, fled to Sudan and then Afghanistan.

The tragedy of Shayma and subsequent messaging is a model for government and community leaders in the aftermath of terrorist attacks today. Instead of giving cold statistics on the 210 Egyptian victims violent extremists killed in the two years prior to this November 1993 attack, the Egyptian media and government humanized one tragic story to drive an irreparable wedge between violent extremists and Egyptian citizens who might have otherwise provided the militants with support or at least passive empathy.

Also, strong counter narratives on wanton

tatarrus should employ imagery. Just as al-Qa`ida uses symbols of Muslim humiliation, Gitmo and Abu Ghraib for example, counter messages should employ images of civilian casualties.

Extremist propaganda presents graphic pictures of Muslim victims of Western attacks, such as victims of drone attacks in Pakistan, to garner support. Popular newspapers in North Africa and the Middle East also publish graphic photographs of these attack victims. Similarly, graphic images of terrorist victims, including women and children, may help further erode support for terrorist tactics. These images must go beyond front page New York Times pictures of suicide attack victims in Iraq. They must go beyond London-based Arabic newspaper Al-Qud's black-and-white photographs of beheaded Iraqis. The images must be burned into the memories of every viewer.

Effective photos do not necessarily have to be bloodier or gorier than al-Qa`ida's images of victims from Western attacks. American film critics widely believe that the most disturbing images from movies are not necessarily gory. The winter breath leaving a murdered Jewish architect in "Schindler's List" and an off-camera ear-carving in "Reservoir Dogs" unsettled moviegoers far more than the explicit violence depicted in any second-rate, gory, B-movie.

Likewise, some of the most influential American photography was not necessarily explicit. National Geographic's photograph of a green-eyed Afghan girl sparked more reader reaction than any gruesome pictures from Russia's war in Afghanistan in the 1980s. A picture of a crying Vietnamese child affected support for the U.S. war in Vietnam more than any battle images.

Al-Qa`ida uses images. Counter-al-Qa`ida campaigns must do the same.

Heretical Devotion to People

Exposing al-Qa`ida and its supporters' hypocritical devotion to radical thinkers will reveal al-Qa`ida's heresy. Despite al-Qa`ida leaders' claims that they adhere only to the original texts of Islam, al-Qa`ida deifies a cadre of ideologues. Such reverence to inspirational intellectuals, or any human being for that matter, is sacrilege to devout Sunnis. And their regard for these ideologues' ideas, while they claim to reject generations of scholarly interpretation of Islam's primary manuscripts, is hypocrisy.

In messages, al-Shabaab, al-Qa`ida in the Arabian Peninsula, and al-Qa`ida in the Islamic Maghrib, for example, will open saying "praise and may God keep Usama bin Ladin" as if bin Ladin were more than a leader—as if he were a demigod. Such praise is flagrantly irreligious to almost any Muslim. In addition, the fact that Usama bin Ladin allows this subservience is narcissistic and equally impious.

Violent radical leaders, by interpreting Islam and how Muslims must act, execute a form of forbidden innovation known as *bid'a*—forbidden innovation of a law or norm.

The Prophet Muhammad said, "I am leaving you two things and you will never go astray as long as you cling to them. They are the Book of Allah and my Sunna [tradition]." Therefore, al-

Qa`ida, who follow books other than those Muhammad clearly promoted, are heretics— incapable of representing or commanding Muslims. Violent extremist followers essentially follow *tawassuf*—the practice of revering religious figures acting as intercessors with God.

Al-Qa`ida leadership and supporters sell themselves as devoted Salafis—those who venerate the first generations of Islam and reject Islamic scholarship, innovation, and interpretations of the Quran and Sunna. Most Salafis seek peaceful religious purity or political action, but al-Qa`ida betrays this faith with their devotion to perverted innovations to justify attacks.

For example, Ibn Taymiyya is still the most influential medieval extremist writer today according to quantitative analysis of citations in extremist leaders' texts and speeches. Ibn Taymiyya justified violence against foreigners. His message still resounds with al-Qa`ida and affiliates worldwide, and he is commonly quoted even on extremist blogs.

Of the modern authors, Sayyid Qutb appears to hold the greatest influence. His commentary on the Quran, along with his seminal book *Milestones*, continues to inspire extremists to act violently. Zawahiri, for example, still openly follows and quotes from Qutb's texts.

Usama Bin Ladin, himself, is one of the top thirteen most influential modern militant authors according to a U.S. Military Academy study.[lxxviii] As the popular icon for a violent united worldwide front, he influences radicals on a global scale.

Dubbing al-Qa`ida followers as "binladinists," "qutbists,"[lxxix] "farajists," and

"taymiyyahists," because they openly praise ideologues such as Sayyid Qutb, Muhammad al-Faraj,
and Ibn Taymiyyah, helps to reveal al-Qa`ida's
blatant hypocrisy.

Extremists are talking out of both sides of
their mouths—touting strict following of the
Quran and Sunna and nothing else, yet also
heretically praising and promoting human beings.

There is no place for cult of personality in
Islam. This simple message will help to staunch
al-Qa`ida growth.

Spiritual Incompetence

Al-Qa`ida leaders lack the religious credentials to
lead, shell out orders, or issue fatwas. Political
and religious leaders representing political entities
wage this criticism against al-Qa`ida almost on a
daily basis. However, credentialed voices who
point out al-Qa`ida's misunderstandings of Islam
remain muted, un-translated, and un-marketed.

Usama bin Ladin was an investor's son
and then militant leader. Ayman al-Zawahiri is a
medical doctor and militant deputy. Each al-
Qa`ida affiliate leader likewise suffers from an
empty space on his resume where religious training and practice might be listed. Some might say
that "true" Salafis only need the Quran and
Hadith without training or critical thought. However, even those Salafis who dispense with
hundreds of years of scholarship still require tutelage, coursework, and practice to apply Islam's
most sacred texts and understand history properly because the texts are not self-evident laws
and recommendations. Even al-Qa`ida leaders ac-

knowledge this vulnerability in their efforts to recruit as many "theologians" as possible to justify
their actions.

Al-Qa`ida's sacred shortcoming is best il-
lustrated in the substance of its essays. For
example, Abu Yahya al-Libi's January 2006 essay
"Tatarrus in Modern Jihad" to justify al-Qa`ida's
murder of tens of thousands of innocent Muslims
to include women, children, elderly, and disabled
persons, is an obvious showcase of religious misunderstanding.

Al-Libi criticizes widely accepted concepts
that civilians are off limits. These mainstream
concepts of "jihad" include strictures on killing
civilians in extreme cases during politically sanctioned warfare:

- When Muslims are on board a ship that
  other Muslims feel they must attack.

- When an enemy uses Muslims literally as
  human shields.

- When an enemy intentionally puts Muslims in a fort or town that is a target for
  other Muslims.

- Innocents must be outright avoided in warfare. (There is contention over this last
  point, because of abrogation of later laws
  to earlier more militant rules, interpretation of the meaning of the Prophet's words
  in different situations, and the relative
  authenticity of different reports of the
  Prophet's words and actions.)

Al-Libi disagrees with these widely accepted rules and claims that modern warfare differs greatly from Muhammad's martial campaign. Therefore, according to al-Libi, old rules should not be applied to contemporary fights. According to al-Libi, today's warfare occurs amid civilians. So for al-Libi, it is permissible and necessary to kill civilians in the process of violent extremist attacks.

Since the essay's publication, Western scholars have pointed out that al-Libi's revisionist interpretation of fighting is an innovation (*bidʾa*)—forbidden in Islam, especially in constructionist Salafi circles in which al-Qaʿida claims to exist. Al-Libi is therefore a hypocrite, according to these scholars.[lxxx]

In reality, this criticism is not quite so black and white since many non-extremist modern Islamic scholars have similarly applied and altered old laws of warfare (and law on other subjects) to new experiences. Nonetheless, stating that killing civilians is permissible is a clear stretch from the basic consensus among most mainstream Muslims that such innocents must be avoided.

Furthermore, al-Libi assumes that warfare has changed significantly, hence the need to change the rules. But raids, guerilla tactics, and small cell attacks that define violent extremist insurgencies today resemble the type of warfare experienced by Muhammad when he faced enemies in deserts and towns who were militarily stronger. The difference is that Muhammad did not egregiously and unnecessarily kill civilians the way al-Qa`ida affiliates do weekly in Iraq, Afghanistan, and Pakistan today.

While these criticisms remain unadvertised, al-Libi's essay has been found on numerous websites to include some al-Qa`ida mainstays such as almedad.com, al-shouraa.com, muslm.net, m3ark.com, shmo5alislam.net, as-ansar.com, majahden.com, hanein.info, and atahadi.com. (By the time this book is published, these web addresses—like other flexible al-Qa`ida-supporting websites—will likely have changed many times over.) Al-Libi's deeply flawed essay enjoys wide marketing. Criticisms of al-Libi's illogical essay do not.

One potentially effective way to deliver the message that al-Qa`ida lacks religious credentials is to paint al-Qa`ida as the widely villainized heretical Islamist group the Khawarij, also known as Kharijites, whom scholars widely consider ignorant about religion. The term can generate visceral repulsion due to the group's infamous reputation in ancient Islamic history.

Based off of available historical sources—and to be fair to the Kharijite sects still in existence—some sects were non-violent and in fact continue to live peacefully today. (When the historical term is popularly used today, it normally refers to the most violent of the Kharijite sects, the Azraqis—puritanical extremists who assassinated Islam's fourth caliph.[lxxxi]) The word Kharijite has become a populist harsh insult.

Today, the group is popularly considered a heretical, perverted enemy in Islamic history. Several governments, including Saudi Arabia and

Indonesia, have used the term to describe terrorists publicly.

Also, as mentioned in the previous chapter, Dr. Qadri has employed the comparison:

> *By undertaking a comprehensive analysis of the signs, beliefs and ideologies of the Khawarij through the Qur'anic verses, Prophetic traditions and jurisprudential opinions of jurists, we have established that the terrorists are the Khawarij of contemporary times.*[lxxxii]

Al-Qa`ida has spent time, money, and manpower to defend against the accusation,[lxxxiii] revealing the power of the insult.

The insulting comparison has some precedent—now a little background. The Kharijites built an independent community in which they claimed to follow the Quran and Sunna strictly and literally. From this base, they waged violent attacks in the name of Allah. They saw the world in black and white. Either one was a devout Muslim who abided by the Kharijite sect's particular version of Islam, or he was an enemy of Allah. Muslims who did not buy into their militant view were condemned to death.

For Kharijites, the ends justified the means. Violence was not just allowed; it was compulsory. Many Muslim scholars consider the Kharijites ignorant of Islam and too quick to judge people as infidels.

Today, al-Qa`ida and its supporters also justify violence against non-Muslims and Muslims who do not adhere to their particular outlook. Al-Qa`ida's ideology resembles the Kharijites in a general way. As one of al-Qa`ida's forefathers Muhammad al-Faraj wrote in his influential book *The Neglected Duty*, "There is no doubt that the idols of this world can only disappear through the power of the sword."

Suicide, murder, mutilation, or anything else is permissible to attain a sprawling Islamic empire ruled under law as defined by the peculiar views of al-Qa`ida, as with the Kharijites. Condemning al-Qa`ida to the Kharijite fringe explains to Muslim communities that terrorists will be condemned to hell.

The argument that modern Kharijites do not follow the way of the Prophet can be an effective counter-voice to al-Qa`ida propaganda.

Likewise, comparing al-Qa`ida to the Qaramita—a fanatical 9th- and 10th-century movement that killed thousands of Muslims in the name of God—will also damage al-Qa`ida's reputation. In a September 2007 statement, top al-Qa`ida lieutenant Abu Yahya al-Libi even admitted that comparisons to the Qaramita would injure al-Qa`ida credibility in the eyes of mainstream Muslims.[lxxxiv]

Messages with these negative comparisons, coming from any Muslim appearing independent of government influence, could help dissuade mainstream Muslims from supporting al-Qa`ida.

And like all messages, they must be accurate, reasoned, and emotive—expressing that al-Qa`ida operates without religious precedent, authority, or knowledge.

Inevitable Failure

Few want to support a lost cause.[lxxxv] So one stream of anti-al-Qa`ida messaging should explain that al-Qa`ida efforts are in vain and ultimately selfishly arrogant, emphasizing in reasoned and practical terms the impossibility of success through violence.

Messages should refute completely any claimed connection between current terrorist tactics and future success, no matter how many generations al-Qa`ida says they plan to attack the West. Messages must show that government security, law enforcement, civilian vigilance, and national confidence are too great.

Al-Qa`ida has consistently justified attacks as the only opportunity for success and has written extensively on the necessity and obligation of violence in reaction to criticism that its cause is lost and therefore self-serving and unholy. Such reactions from al-Qa`ida underline the potential success of counter-messaging that al-Qa`ida's tactics are destined to fail.

Some ideologues supporting al-Qa`ida spend their careers mainly focused on the necessity of violence as the only means, as explained in the chapter on al-Qa`ida ideology. Examples are Faraj's aforementioned treatise and Anwar al-Awlaki's most popular online essays (available on dozens of sites). Awlaki's lecture "Constants on the Path of Jihad," for example, persuades Muslims toward violence in no uncertain terms. His "44 Ways of Supporting Jihad" commands every Muslim to focus every resource and effort toward violence against Western and secular governments at all times without reprieve. Within 24 hours of the essay's posting in January 2009, it received over 1,000 downloads, and 61 other websites had already reposted the text.[lxxxvi]

Al-Qa`ida stresses that the movement of violence will continue long after leaders' deaths.[lxxxvii] Bin Ladin and all his deputies are openly aware of their mortality. And fighters have gladly died with the knowledge that success would be certain—even if it takes generations. Foreign and Iraqi fighters willingly remained in Fallujah, Iraq in November 2004 knowing they would die as Marines surrounded and entered the town. Insurgents near al-Qa'im, on the border with Syria, holed up in the basements of houses to die fighting Americans in July 2005.[lxxxviii] They believed that they were one piece of a greater fight that would last perhaps centuries before victory.

However, take any possibility of future victory away and new recruits are more likely to grow doubts about dying for a dying cause.

Thus far, continued counterterrorism military and police policies do not appear to substantially drain the morale of terrorists. The terrorist plots continue. Messages must, therefore, aggressively drill the fact into the minds of Muslims that failure is inevitable: a hundred or a thousand generations of violence in the name of God against the United States and West will not bring a restored Islamic empire.

Failed Governance

Banna, Qutb, Faraj, Fadl (before his recantation), Zawahiri, Ladin, and all of al-Qa`ida's major influencers, ideologues, and tactical leaders lack any clear vision for the future. While they might say "Islam is the answer" and might claim to want an "Islamic state" with "Islamic law," al-Qa`ida militants and spokesmen fail to define any of these concepts. The luxury of opposition—those not in power—is that they can criticize without the burden of actually ruling. With no power comes no responsibility. Once in power, the opposition suddenly has to clarify and implement formerly dreamy and unspecific promises. And power then inevitably requires some level of compromise and in turn then inspires new dissenting classes of citizenry.

Even if al-Qa`ida were ever to come to power or inspire like-minded individuals to rule over a significant amount of land over a long period of time, these rulers would fail as evidenced by past al-Qa`ida behavior. For a few moments in a few areas, al-Qa`ida affiliates have governed and have failed. In Fallujah—before U.S. Marines and Soldiers rid the city of terrorists—binladinists threw away music CDs, beheaded rumored secularists, and grew beards instead of offering real government for real people with real needs.

Al-Qa`ida's sister organization, the Taliban, claimed to "govern" Afghanistan in the 1990s and continue to contest bits of land. But destroying graves, stoning women, and cutting off the hands of thieves took precedence over education, usable roads, agricultural aid, and the common missions of any serious government.

Somalia's al-Shabaab—who publicly claim allegiance to al-Qa`ida—also allot harsh punishments without regard to the actual fair governance of Somalis in southern Somalia, where they rule as of this book's printing in summer 2010.

In short, al-Qa`ida cannot govern. If in a parallel universe al-Qa`ida were to create their imaginary caliphate, it would be a bad joke of anti-governance. People, no matter how devout, would be miserable and could only allow such existence for so long. If these stories of failed governance were told today—before al-Qa`ida has a chance to gain more land—passive Muslim communities might be more likely to abandon apathy for activism against al-Qa`ida.

Beyond this revealed inability to govern, al-Qa`ida's unspecific "Islamic law" by definition is human law. Human interpretation and human implementation (subject at all times to human reason and human error) make this "Islamic law" by definition secular law. In short, al-Qa`ida's implementation of law is unholy by its own standard of insisting on the law of God only. This logic undermines the fabric of al-Qa`ida and all its predecessor ideologues such as Qutb and Faraj who called for strict adherence to "Islamic law."

Furthermore, al-Qa`ida's dreamed "restored Islamic Caliphate" that is supposed to have once spanned Muslim communities from East Asia to Western Europe was never a homogenous international Islamic community. Even Muhammad's successors, the Ummayads, and then the Abbasids faced continual internal strife, civil war, and melding with many different ethnicities, cultures, histories, governments, and religious interpretations among the societies over which these empires held limited and sometimes contested administrative rule. Islamic empires, like all powers in history, had to balance ideals

with practical solutions and compromise and con-
tend with inevitable opposition and
revolutionaries. An empire today would face the
same challenges. Al-Qa`ida cannot deliver a para-
dise on earth.

Unholy Certainty

Mainstream Muslim and non-Muslim scholars
have maintained for centuries that there is limited
ambiguity within the Islamic texts on which religious law is based. Both the Quran and Hadith
hold disputed and unclear language, enough to
undermine attempts of non-scholars (such as al-
Qa`ida leaders) to make absolutist statements on
religious law.

     Muslim scholars have traditionally ended
their assessments with the words "God knows
best" to emphasize both the limits of human reason and the inherent uncertainties in some of the
original texts of Islam.

     These ambiguities, according to scores of
scholars from all of Islam's schools of thought as
well as Western intellectuals, include:[lxxxix]

- Although the Quran holds about 500
  verses of direct legal content (requiring little interpretation even today), the Quran
  used today was written down from careful
  oral recitations and memorization well after Muhammad's death. Ultimately it was a
  human endeavor—with many political as
  well as well-meaning pious interests and
  influences resulting in multiple written
  versions at one point in Islam's second

generation.

- There were contestations over the order in which the Quran's chapters and verses were written. The Quran was not necessarily written in the order the Prophet spoke. Order is important because it is widely understood that later texts abrogate earlier statements for religious laws as well as less formal custom recommendations. Uncertainty of order translates into some uncertainty of laws and customs to include laws of warfare.

- Many years passed before an accepted version of the Quran was voweled, since the original Quran did not have vowel marks, which could, in some cases, cause more than one interpretation of a statement or word. There are volumes of scholarly works (even today) debating meaning and grammar of words, phrases, and concepts in the Quran.

- Words—such as the word for "power"—and general terms may be inherently ambiguous and may require some form of human interpretation.

- Analogies and general statements abound in the Quran and necessarily require judgment and some interpretation—even for constructionist and literalist modern-day Salafis.

- Hadith scholarship requires analysis of both the substance of a statement (*matn*) and the veracity of those in the line of oral transmitters (*isnad*). No scholar accepts all Hadith as correct and veracious, and some scholars accept under a dozen Hadith statements depending on which methodology is used to interpret a Hadith's substance and transmitters. Debate and critical scholarship will never end over each Hadith, as evidenced even in contemporary academia.

Verses on "jihad"—which al-Qa`ida interprets—are riddled with ambiguities. An effective competing narrative, therefore, could focus on the innate uncertainties over the texts, which al-Qa`ida leaders quote without critical thought. These uncertainties are inconsistent with al-Qa`ida's absolutist and overly confident claims that followers must fight, die, and kill civilians in the name of al-Qa`ida's leaders.

Al-Qa`ida leaders do not exhibit the common reverence and modesty mainstream religious leaders and scholars display. While scholars and leaders openly admit the limits of human interpretation and state "God knows best," al-Qa`ida ideologues and leaders brazenly speak in absolutes with regard to violence and killing civilians.

Threat to Tribal Construct

Al-Qa`ida and tribes are incompatible.

Al-Qa`ida's goal is an imagined unspecified transnational caliphate of "equal" citizens subjugated under a caliph. This aim, by definition, precludes tribalism. Al-Qa`ida is therefore a threat to tribes.

Al-Qa`ida's anti-tribal penchant can help to inspire counter-al-Qa`ida movements the world over. Its ill-informed anti-clan stance was starkly highlighted in Iraq, where tribalism is arguably the strongest social construct. Since tribes survived Genghis Khan and Alexander the Great's anti-tribal policies, al-Qa`ida's intent in Iraq reeks of egregious hubris.

In some ways, even today, Iraq is more an area where tribes live than a nation. Today, at least three quarters of those who live in Iraq are bound to one of the 150 tribes. Most others associate themselves with one of these clans.

How did the tribal structures survive Saddam's despotic regime? And how will they, again, survive al-Qa`ida and other outside influence? Saddam Hussein actually encouraged tribalism. After failing to cement his regime by promoting nationalism, Islam, and the Mesopotamia legacy, the dictator decided to pay off tribes to solidify support and strengthen his personal security.

Saddam promoted tribalism when he felt he had lost his grip on Iraq. First, in the last couple of years of the Iran-Iraq war, Saddam sensed that Iraqis, especially those shedding blood for the seemingly endless and pointless war, were greatly discouraged with the regime. To drum up support, Saddam bribed sheikhs, who in turn pledged their loyalty to the president. Furthermore, to encourage tribalism, he applauded soldiers' tribes when he toured the trenches. In the final years of the

Iran-Iraq war, Saddam woke up to the political reality of Iraqi society.

Again, in the days and years after the Gulf War, Saddam realized that to earn any semblance of public support he once again had to turn to the tribes. The Gulf War ruined Iraq's infrastructure and left Iraqis in despair. To pour salt on the wound that was Iraq, Saddam drove his Republican Guard forces through the southern provinces, annihilating the post-Gulf War rebellion. But once he had laid his hammer down, Saddam needed to change roles and shore up some backing.

The despot again paid sheikhs for support. He increased payments for crops from tribal properties. Also, in tribal areas he built schools and hospitals and allowed tribal leaders to decide on criminal cases. Throughout much of the south, Saddam set up houses where his representatives could hold discussions with sheikhs. Saddam even provided clan leadership with smuggled cars.

For these gifts, Saddam Hussein demanded loyalty. Individual sheikhs had to express their devotion verbally to his representatives. In 1992, Saddam had 586 tribal sheikhs give an oath to the government. Beyond these pledges, many tribes acted as Baghdad's army in far off areas so that Saddam could avoid spreading his forces thin throughout Iraq. He gave clans light arms, howitzers, mortars, and RPGs. With the weapons, tribes patrolled streets in urban areas, charged tolls, and inspected vehicles driving to and from Syria and Jordan. The autocrat successfully built a symbiosis between tribes and the government, thus bolstering his personal security.

Saddam Hussein was not the first to exploit the power of the tribes. The Ottoman Empire, at first wishing to bind communities through only Islam, eventually sent representatives to confer directly with the sheikhs around Basra, Baghdad, and Mosul. When the British enthroned Faisal I, the King governed largely through the tribal leaders. The monarchies, military, and Baathist governments of the twentieth century alike set aside dreams of a "modern"-looking nation for political realism. Even the oil boom of the 1970s, producing wealth and an intellectual revival, failed to alter Iraqi society. In 2006, tribes joined to fight al-Qa`ida elements as part of the Anbar Awakening, and to this day tribal politics are often synonymous with (or at least echo in) Iraqi local, provincial, and national politics.

The bottom line is that tribalism was deeply ingrained in Iraqi culture. And al-Qa`ida's attempt to subjugate tribes was a strategic mistake. Like in Iraq, tribes are important cultural and social constructs in Somalia, North Africa, the Sahel, Yemen, Afghanistan, and western Pakistan—all areas with al-Qa`ida presence. And as in Iraq, violent extremist efforts to check tribal power will likely lead to al-Qa`ida's demise. Explaining what happened in Iraq may offer awareness and inspiration to anti-al-Qa`ida movements throughout ungoverned tribal territories where al-Qa`ida militants prey.

The similar survival of Afghan tribes—in the face of brutal anti-tribal strategies and political sidelining over the past half century—attests to their strength, longevity, and resilience.

Before the Soviets invaded Afghanistan, Afghan kings relied on tribal and sub-tribal leaders to enforce laws and security. The Soviets in the late 1970s, however, viewed tribes as antiquated, socially regressive, and a possible threat to central political leadership. The government executed hundreds of tribal and clan leaders and important members in an attempt to stem tribal influence. But the tribal system remained.

During the 1980s, the "mujahadin"—both foreigners and Afghans—attempted to circumnavigate tribes to follow only those they believed to be ideological and theological leaders of the religiously inspired resistance. But the tribal system remained.

In the 1990s, the Taliban viewed the tribal system as hostile to religion and the Taliban's ruling structure. The Taliban thus sidelined the tribal leaders and filled national, provincial, and municipal positions with Taliban "clerics." But the tribal system remained.

Since 2001, Taliban insurgents have assassinated tribal leaders and key members aligning themselves with the central government. But the tribal system remains.

Terrorism analysts and regional experts, historians, and sociologists have argued that Afghanistan's tribal system may be weak or may have gone through a period of decline. However, the system's very existence through millennia of outside and central government rule demonstrates its resiliency and strength.

Even the deaths of hundreds of tribal and tribal-confederacy leaders have not stopped the tribes from growing strong enough for the current

Kabul administration—no matter how corrupt and limited in power—to acknowledge and work with in an attempt to implement law and security.

Therefore, central to any marketing campaign in Afghanistan (and amplified throughout the world) to delegitimize the Taliban and al-Qa`ida, and attempt to inspire opposition to violent extremists, will be underlining that violent extremist presence, by definition, threatens all tribal systems.

Al-Qa`ida will often attempt to endear itself to some tribes when its elements first move to an area, as al-Qa`ida in the Arabian Peninsula does in Yemen through intermarriage, money, and arms-as-gifts. This initial kindness occurs only as long as al-Qa`ida is still building a safe haven area to conduct planning or training. But the moment al-Qa`ida moves to govern an area—with Afghanistan, southern Somalia, and 2004 Fallujah as examples of temporary governance—al-Qa`ida tries to destroy the tribal system. If tribes are aware of this before al-Qa`ida shows up, tribal leaders may be more apt to repel the initial wave of violent extremist influence.

Hindrance to Aid

Another counter narrative is the insecurity al-Qa`ida brings to its contested regions, preventing aid from reaching areas of need. This practical and immediate counter-message is illustrated most bluntly in Yemen, which faces the world's gravest water crisis (along with volumes of other health, agricultural, financial, and security challenges). In Yemen, aid groups will not go near areas where al-Qa`ida in the Arabian Peninsula militants may reside or operate—thus al-Qa`ida is sealing off communities from sustainable potable water sources.

The indications of Yemen's water crisis are alarming:

- At the current rate, according to dozens of independent studies, Yemen will be the first nation to literally run out of water in the next decade. And that does not take into account more and more refugees, an increasing qat trade which sucks up about 40 percent of Yemen's water, further droughts, and a growing population, which will speed this catastrophe.[xc] [xci] [xcii] [xciii]

- Each Yemeni has access to only 125 cubic meters per person per year of water compared with the regional average of ten times that. [xciv] [xcv] [xcvi] [xcvii]

- The World Bank reports that only 44 percent of the population has access to water supplies and only 12 percent to safe drinkable water.[xcviii] [xcix] [c]

- In urban areas, during planned water outages, families are forced to pay up to two thirds of their income to purchase potable water from roving water trucks.[ci] [cii] [ciii] [civ]

- In the countryside and mountainous areas, tribes send out search parties to find new springs because the local wells have run dry.[cv] [cvi]

- In the Sana`a basin, water was reachable at 20 meters but now cannot be found at 200 meters underground.[cvii] [cviii] [cix] [cx]

Despite this humanitarian disaster, aid cannot reach many areas of Yemen because aid groups, with good reason, will not go near militant-heavy tribal areas in eastern Yemen.

If foreign companies, non-profits, and government construction and surveyors cannot work in impermissible environs, communities have great reason to revolt against al-Qa`ida. Highlighting this humanitarian insecurity can be a mainstay of a robust online media campaign to undermine al-Qa`ida's ability to influence future recruits and supporters.

The message could be as simple as "no al-Qa`ida presence equals aid," or "al-Qa`ida presence equals no aid."

Al-Qa`ida Brings War

Another potentially potent message to undermine al-Qa`ida credibility and possibly inspire communities to speak out against and even fight violent extremists is that "al-Qa`ida brings war." Without al-Qa`ida and the Taliban—despite what conspiracy-theorist pundits state about U.S. aspirations for global dominance—the U.S. and allied militaries and heavy-handed Arab government police tactics would recede.

Usama bin Ladin and Ayman al-Zawahiri need the appearance of a seismic religious war to be relevant—to be listened to. To maintain credibility as inspirers of a global insurgency, they need to be targets of the United States—to be enemies resembling the Soviet Union as an existential violent threat to "America" and the "American way of life" and the "West" and the "Western way of life."

So al-Qaʿida attacks Western targets and then waits to receive its Western reprisal in the form of drone attacks, U.S. forces, NATO commands, or, by proxy, secular Arab police. Then al-Qaʿida can continue its unnecessary war, which has no chance of victory.

When affiliates take on the name "al-Qaʿida" such as al-Qaʿida in the Lands of the Islamic Maghrib (transnational insurgents in North Africa, who use al-Qaʿida's name with its permission for international recognition and credibility), this action alone warrants police and military attention. It is unfortunate that the U.S. and other Western governments play into al-Qaʿida's hands and actually use the names al-Qaʿida affiliates dub themselves. Such recognition plays further into the fantasy of cosmic war al-Qaʿida leaders need to survive and remain in the annals of modern history. (It would be a wiser policy for governments NEVER to use the names al-Qaʿida affiliates use for themselves—instead governments could call an organization "bin Ladinists in North Africa" for example.)

Because the West will inevitably avenge attacks; because Western reprisal, especially when it involves allied militaries in Afghanistan for the first decade of the twenty-first century, will reek havoc on local Muslim communities; and because reprisal will mean civilian deaths both from Western militaries and al-Qa`ida's ensuing counter-counter attacks, Muslims have every reason to squash any burgeoning al-Qa`ida influence.

If a Muslim community wants to avoid drone attacks, a Western invasion, or local police crackdowns, it is in the community's best interest to eviscerate al-Qa`ida before it can become strong enough to gain recognition from the West—in words or actions.

This message of "al-Qa`ida brings war"—if marketed accurately using statistics from Afghanistan on the number of U.S. troops there and if marketed emotively to incite apathetic Muslims to give a damn—has the potential to help inspire community leaders to drive an irreparable wedge between violent extremists and would-be future recruits and supporters.

These counter-narrative streams are just some messages that may help to justify those actively fighting al-Qa`ida, inspire apathetic communities to activate against al-Qa`ida influence, dissuade potential violent extremists, and put al-Qa`ida on the defensive. As specified in the last chapter, these argument streams are best delivered from the mouths and pens of credentialed independent religious leaders, former militants, and terrorism victims. But local, unknown, or anonymous messengers—using the themes in this chapter—may have an effect.

14. TRANSLATION: LABORIOUS AND NECESSARY

Just as al-Qa`ida and al-Qa`ida-affiliate marketers translate their radical literature and speeches into other languages quickly and accurately, translators must accurately translate counter-al-Qa`ida messages.

The importance of translation is highlighted in the radicalization of Mohammad Sidique Khan, mastermind of the 7 July 2005 attacks on London's subway. According to his brother, Khan could not relate to the local non-violent imam because of the language barrier. Khan spoke English. The imam taught only in Urdu and Arabic.[cxi]

In the future, people like Khan should have access to counter-al-Qa`ida ideas in clear English (or in their native tongues). Translations must include African, European, and Southeast and Southwest Asian languages: Modern Standard Arabic, Bahasa Indonesia, Bahasa Melayu, French (of France), Pashto, Urdu, Farsi, Bosanski, Chechen, Turkish, Kurdish, Tagalog, Afsoomaali, German, Spanish (of Latin America), Dutch, Hindi, Chinese (simplified), Thai, and Tamil for starters. Al-Qa`ida narratives are found in all these languages.

Of the three stages (Identify, Translate, and Market) of this book's solution to end al-Qa`ida, this part is the most expensive, time consuming, and underestimated.

Unfortunately, there is no cheap silver bullet. Translation is a skill picked up through a lifetime of study and practice. A quality translator is not just bilingual, but a literary critic, poet, and essayist with a wealth of real-world and critical editorial experience. And no computer will ever replace a translator. Practically speaking, this means that translations for the campaign described in this book will cost millions.

Even online databases that include billions of phrases with the best statistical models and most sophisticated statistical machine translation software will fail to approach what a talented translator can produce. For example, a machine will never accurately portray tone or sarcasm.

Even the world's best online translation service—Google, in my experience—cannot stand up to a living translator. It is true that Google has been a trailblazer in creating its own state-of-the-art translation technology. Specifically, the company uses statistical analysis for translation, which often yields more accurate translations than less flexible simple word-based, phrase-based, and syntax-based technology—the latter three techniques will not accurately interpret idioms, for example. Google applies Franz Och's (a technology and translation pioneer) algorithm to prioritize possible translations from one source-language text (using a database of millions of already-recorded translations) and subsequently chooses the "best" translations.

Google also uses "crowd-sourcing," whereby the company pairs volunteer translators to translation needs. Even so, Google Translate can only be used as a tool to understand a text and cannot replace a thoughtful and critical translator who understands flow, syntax, structure, and culture.[cxii]

I submitted only one full page (485 words) of text from a New York Times article devoid of any specialized or technical vocabulary (twelve-point font, single spaced, Times New Roman font) to top human translation services who use qualified translators and qualified reviewers (to double-check work and offer further expertise). I asked each company how much it would cost to translate the text from English to each of the aforementioned twenty languages. Here were my responses on 21 April 2010 (the companies asked not to be named)[14]:

---

[14] Company 1: $105 USD per language in three days (Total Translation Cost -- $2,100)

Company 2: Modern Standard Arabic -- $175.00, Bahasa Indonesia -- $185.00, Bahasa Melayu [Malay] -- $185.00, French -- $150.00, Pashto -- $185.00, Urdu -- $185.00, Farsi -- $185.00, Turkish -- $165.00, Tagalog -- $175.00, German -- $150.00, Spanish -- $110.00, Dutch -- $175.00, Hindi -- $185.00, Chinese -- $175.00 [Traditional or Simplified Chinese], Thai -- $185.00, Tamil -- $185.00, Bosanski/Hrvatski -- [language not served], Chechen -- [language not served], Afsoomaali -- [language not served], Kurdish -- [language not served] in four-five days (Total Translation Cost for only 16 of the 20 languages -- $2,775)

Company 3: Modern Standard Arabic -- $125.00, Bahasa Indonesia -- $135.00, Bahasa Melayu -- $135.00, French -- $125.00, Pashto -- $125.00, Urdu -- $135.00, Farsi --

- Company 1: $2,100.00 USD.
- Company 2: $2,775.00 USD (with four languages not served).
- Company 3: $2,782.50 USD.

$125.00, Bosanski/Hrvatski-- $125.00, Chechen --$150.00, Turkish -- $125.00, Kurdish -- $150.00, Tagalog -- $150.00, Afsoomaali -- $145.00, German -- $125.00, Spanish -- $90.00, Dutch -- $135.00, Hindi --$135.00, Chinese -- $125.00, Thai -- $145.00, Tamil -- $145.00 in 2-3 days (Total Translation Cost -- $2,650.00, with administrative fee -- $2,782.50)

15. AMPLIFICATION

Websites with counter-al-Qa`ida messages should super-saturate the Internet with sound bites, powerful quotes, pictures, and promotion of sources' credentials and independence.

Anonymity

Sites may use anonymous host servers (plenty in the United States, Canada, Malaysia, Hong Kong, and Europe—the same that al-Qa`ida uses) for the safety of the executors of this book's proposal. Some may fear that al-Qa`ida could still track down the website creators even when the site host uses a reputable anonymizing service. However, if the U.S. and other Western governments are unable to track down the sources of mainstay al-Qa`ida websites, it is unlikely that al-Qa`ida would be able to track down a legal site using the best legal anonymizers. This is not to underestimate al-Qa`ida's technical acumen but to allay fears of reprisal for those wishing to execute this plan.

    Some may argue that Internet anonymity may make users uncomfortable—perhaps viewers might assume a website is government-run and therefore the site might not be trusted as independent. And if a government program were actually behind an anonymous site and this information were uncovered somehow, then some might think the media could have a field day over a government's effort to not only produce propaganda but also to hide anonymously—such a scenario could reek of conspiracy in the headlines. However, anonymous website hosting is so common that making a site anonymous is no longer strange or newsworthy. Anonymous services are not only common among businesses and non-profits; they are good professional practice: offering the site creators personal security and the business as a whole (especially if the site is linked into a company database or server) corporate security.

Furthermore, there should never be a need for unnecessary controversy (unless you think the controversy will help skyrocket the counter narratives without undermining their impact) because this book's plan calls for no propaganda—the strategy is simply amplification of messages that already exist. This effort does not curb freedom of speech and is not tantamount to psychological operations. It is only boosting counter-al-Qa`ida voices.

Also, sites must be designed for search engine optimization to ensure they appear first during searches and drown out al-Qa`ida propaganda.

Recent marketing research suggests the following steps to allow a website to gain higher rankings during online searches, which could be applied to those trying to amplify counter-violence messages:

Blogging/Websites

- Publish blog/website content everywhere possible.

- Videos should be published on Viddler, Blip.tv, Revver, Youtube, and Tubearoo.

- Blog/Website article titles should be either alluring (such as lists like "list of 5 things to avoid to go to heaven," "don't read this," "no one should see this," "enter at own risk") or made to maximize keyword searches (such as "Egyptian Counter Violence Book").

- To maintain readership, add content 1–3 times per week.

- Possible content: publish counter-violence statements, statements about the competing narrative authors, or lists of other websites' links and articles with comments.

Search Engine Optimization (SEO)[15]

- Content.

  - o   Words that will help people on search engines find your website.

  - o   Keywords in URL (website title).

  - o   Keywords in headings and in bold text.

  - o   Keywords in website description—unique words and unique description for each page of each website which are submitted to search engine companies.

  - o   "SEO video" gives sites "a 53 times better chance of getting to Page 1 Google ranking" according to Forrester Research. The method is to submit videos themselves—not as a link to a video sharing website and not as a feature on a webpage—to various search engines using XML tools. The video should be "optimized" just like with a webpage:

---

[15] Search Engine Optimization (SEO) is the process of increasing traffic to a website from search engines by unpaid search results. Generally, search engine optimization helps a website to appear earlier on an online search.

keywords and phrases for searching should be used in the file name, captions, and titles.[cxiii] Reportedly, this methodology helps to improve SEO because search engines are now using "blended" search engine results to include pictures, videos, articles, and multiple other sections of the web content itself. Video content has less competition because currently very little online video is submitted to search engines separately.

- Links

  o Have other websites post links to your site, especially trusted popular sources (such as CNN, al-Jazira, al-Quds online), by effective marketing and getting your site mentioned in the news cycle.

Social Media Marketing

- Become an active member of online communities before promoting material—socialize yourself comfortably before socializing your site and your messages.

- Promote: 1) your articles 2) your videos 3) content about your articles and videos posted by other people/entities.

- Maximize social media tools on your website, such as Facebook, Twitter, Reddit, Digg, Del.icio.us, StumbleUpon, Technorati, Ning, Furl, Ma.gnolia, and Mixx.

This way viewers can "tag" your webpage to a wider audience.

Analyze success

- Use Google Reader, Digg, Hubspot, or Alexa to monitor views and outside links to each of your blogs or websites.

- You can also assess how searchable your articles and websites are by searching for them yourself.

In summary:

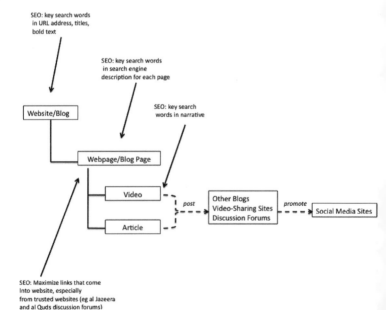

Any online competing narrative campaign should take advantage of the latest free online marketing techniques to ensure that websites appear first to community and religious leaders searching for information to inoculate communities against al-Qa`ida propaganda. Non violent-extremist supporting websites have the advantage that they can more openly advertise on online social networks and submit searchable terms to search engine companies without fear of government retribution. In contrast, operational security hinders al-Qa`ida-supporting sites in conducting maximal online marketing. Bottom line: non-violent sites have the advantage.

Also, websites should be searchable—and ahead of al-Qa`ida-supporting sites in online searches—by the same terms al-Qa`ida uses. For example, non-violent sites should be searchable by terms such as "Guantanamo," "Iraq," "Palestine," "Afghanistan," "Abu Ghraib"—terms al-Qa`ida uses to hook in audiences and would-be supporters and recruits. By mirroring al-Qa`ida's search terms, competing narratives can play a direct counterpoint to al-Qa`ida propaganda and help to build doubt in those on the fence ideologically.

Just as al-Qa`ida began with its online ideology library al-Tawhid to get all the world's militants on a single page concerning permissibility of violence against civilians and Muslim governments, an online counter-al-Qa`ida information operations campaign is a necessary start. The Internet offers the flexibility, anonymity, and instant worldwide reach required to undermine a fluid transnational insurrection.

Offline Competing Narratives

Although the Internet should be the first (and by far most important) place to disseminate counter-al-Qa`ida messaging, the next step would be to look toward physical literature, word of mouth, television, text messaging, and radio. Since the Internet does not reach everywhere—especially impoverished and ungoverned territories such as rural Afghanistan and many areas of the Sahara— the same messages on the Internet should be available via these traditional media and word-of-mouth networks such as tribe and mosque networks. If the Internet message is evocative enough—employing the strategy of using emotive and accurate messages from credentialed independent sources—the message will naturally have a viral effect from the virtual to the real world. In other words, an online message would ideally affect sermons in mosques and radio discussions alike.

To further this effect, governments (anonymously) or independent publishers and producers wishing to counter al-Qa`ida should be encouraged to actively replay and echo online messages against violent extremism offline. And physical literature, television, and radio amplifying counter-violence narratives are legal compared with al-Qa`ida's non-internet media, which can only be distributed sparingly in the darkness of night and via temporary radio towers quickly taken down by governments. Bottom line: counter-al-Qa`ida messages on traditional media have the legal advantage over al-Qa`ida.

Of special note is the popularity of radio in ungoverned areas. A rewarding investment for any person, nongovernment organization, or government entity might be to give rudimentary radio equipment (reaching a limited area) to any tribal or religious leader with anti-al-Qa`ida sentiments—as long as this person has personal protection from violent extremist retribution. Alternatively, ungoverned areas' religious and tribal leaders may be given cell or satellite phones to call into regional radio stations that would be interested in amplifying counter-violence statements.

Nonetheless, and this point cannot be stressed enough, al-Qa`ida focuses on the Internet for a reason: it reaches the most people most cheaply most securely. Likewise, a counter-al-Qa`ida information campaign should first and foremost play on this same battlefield to drown out violent propaganda. Traditional media efforts would be only icing on the cake. And traditional media, in some communities, may be outright assumed to be government-run—undermining a message's effectiveness. The Internet is the first and most important road for counter narratives, but traditional media should not be ignored.

Marketing Forums

Offline and online competing narratives may sometimes be best delivered in emotive and evocative formats—for example in the form of comics, cartoons, humor, acerbic sarcasm, beauty, sexuality, and controversy to draw in unengaged communities. These entertaining venues and motifs may help to spark conversation, and to inspire previously apathetic community leaders and youth to repel violent extremist literature, online propaganda, and al-Qa`ida-inspired recruiters.

Comics

"The 99" comic book series tells a story of 99 superheroes from around the world who combat villains—succeeding only when they work together. Its creator, psychologist and part-time Kuwait/part-time U.S. resident Naif al-Mutawa, explained to media that, "there is no religion in the story line" but instead "basic human values like trust and generosity." He explained that, "the comics explore shared values more than individual religious experiences." However, Mutawa did study the Quran for inspiration for his storylines and characters.

One of his latest issues takes place in the Philippines where the "99" fight the villainous "Death Merchant," who is attacking an international relief agency. This story's exposition appears similar to real world scenarios in which al-Qa`ida elements keep aid groups from reaching people in need. Examples are the Taliban in western Pakistan and al-Shabaab in southern Somalia.

The comic book is printed in eight languages and distributed as widely as India, China, and the United States. This priority put on translation should be an example of excellence for competing networks attempting to reach the widest audiences possible.

Detracting from the comic book's potential to reach wider audiences is the U.S. President's open praise for the author and series during April

2010's Summit on Entrepreneurship. Although the praise earned media attention, Western praise may tarnish the veneer of independence to those distrustful of the West.

Cartoons

Somali-Canadian satirical cartoonist Amin Amir has gained popularity over the past decade with his cartoons depicting violent extremists' negative impacts on Somalia and government corruption.

His cartoons have earned him death threats from extremists, and Puntland's (a Somali province) president threatened to sue Amir for libel in 2008. Amir has also received prizes and grants in Canada for his artwork.

The media attention from his critics along with his evocative and imaginative cartoons have helped his website aminarts.com to receive over 10,000 hits per day and attain a worldwide reach, according to an online website tracking service. Viewership is most common in E.U. countries with large Somali Diasporas.

Amir's cartoons against violent extremists have the potential to resonate everywhere—not just in Somalia and Somali Diaspora communities—while his anti-Somali-government stance makes him appear independent of the internationally backed Somali Transitional Federal Government. His cartoons appear to focus on concern for ordinary citizens and have the potential to highlight vulnerabilities and inconsistencies in al-Shabaab's narrative and actions. The cartoons succinctly and entertainingly reveal violent extremists' unconcern for innocents.

Comedy

Talasim (talasim.com) is an online comedy community for Arabic-speaking persons founded in 2009. Talasim has a network of interactive content-producers and original comedic content from over 25 countries—to include religious and political humor. One of the founders described the company as a "humoristic and realistic approach to help Arab youth express themselves in a more spontaneous manner."

The 2009 "6th Investing in Technology Forum" in Egypt selected Talasim as one of the Arab world's top ten investment-ready startup companies—further boosting publicity.

This online vehicle for Arabic-language expression may help young people to express their opinions and frustrations candidly and may offer an alternative to violent extremist blogs and similar web forums.

Satire in Film and Theater

According to a UK think tank[cxiv], sardonic comedies can serve to deflate al-Qa`ida's attraction to some Muslim communities. The report claims that some violent extremists are akin to "counter-cultural, subversive groups of predominantly angry young men" and that "being radical and rebelling against the received values of the status quo is an important part of being young."

Jamie Bartlett, one of the report's authors, stated, "For a minority, al-Qaeda might seem a 'cool' gang to join, even though the truth is that its members are ignorant and incompetent. This does not make it any less serious or dangerous. Terror-ist activity amounts, all too often, to teenage kicks that kill."

According to the study, satire may tear any romance away from al-Qa`ida's brand name. For example, "Jihad! The Musical" and the movie "Four Lions" attempt to showcase violent philoso-phy's weaknesses in a venue which some young people (the ones this study believes are attracted to extremism) could appreciate.

It must be noted that there is no evidence that youthful rebellion is a key radicalization driver, but satire may still be an effective medium for delivering competing narratives.

The following three examples are not counter-extremist narratives but public service non-profit messages that went "viral"—they gained a large viewership without high-priced advertise-ment. Counter-narrative efforts should learn from viral marketing successes. Although it is impossi-ble to predict viral potential prior to campaign inception—even with focus groups—counter-narrative strategies may find that beauty, sexual-ity, and controversy may help to amplify credible voices virally.

Beauty

The United Kingdom published a video "Embrace Life" as part of a seatbelt-wearing campaign. Al-though certainly not a counter-al-Qa`ida message, the effort can inform a messaging campaign. The

video (http://www.youtube.com/watch?v=h-8PBx
7isoM) shows a wife and daughter's arms acting
as a seatbelt for a man in an imaginary car accident. There is no dialogue, just music.

The video—likely through word of mouth
and online links—received an online viewership of
over one million almost immediately after its 29
January 2010 publication and doubled that
within a month. Some have considered the video
to be so emotive that religious groups have reposted the video and mainstream press have
covered both the viral and substantive nature of
the video—likely leading to even greater awareness
and viewership for the advertisement.

Sexuality

A 2010 breast cancer awareness ad to promote a
Canadian charity and target young people quickly
went viral on popular video sharing websites
(http://www.youtube.com/watch?v=8tkB264wZZ
k). The video, which viewers have described as
tastefully racy and humorous, quickly made
mainstream Western headlines for its ribaldry and
wit. The advertisement was so well received that
cancer awareness and fundraising organization
leaders were invited onto talk shows to discuss
the video—giving these non-profit representatives
a platform on which to discuss serious issues.

In short, the advertisement's sexual content helped skyrocket viewership and led to media
stories, which further increased audiences. In addition, organizational principals received press
attention to further their goals of public awareness.

Controversy

In France, the Association for Nonsmoker's Rights published three photographs in 2010 as part of a marketing campaign "meant to shock...to reach young people" according to the organization. The suggestive images—showing young persons in a position as if to give oral sex to older men in business suits (perhaps meant to portray tobacco executives)—display the words "Smoking means being a slave to tobacco."

Before the advertisements were even used in France, media stories on the controversy displayed the pictures. The free promotion has been so widespread that the association announced there would not be a need to buy magazine space as originally intended.

Adding to the controversy and possibly increasing viewership, France's Family Minister Nadine Morano stated the campaign may "constitute an affront to public decency" because of the "disrespectful" and "provocative" nature of the pictures. Controversy made the ads go super-viral.

Looking to the future, a new technology or new medium may eclipse this entire chapter. Advancements in communications platforms and technology accelerate at a breakneck speed, and in a matter of weeks or months, new venues—online and offline—may make the suggestions in this chapter antiquated. So a key question for any marketer is how to keep a step ahead of al-Qa`ida—so we are not just copying al-Qa`ida's marketing methodologies but leading instead.

One answer—looking to what technologies and communications will prevail in the future—would be to look to the pornography industry.[16] The pornography industry has been at the helm of communications technologies for the past 115 years. The industry has often foretold what media tools would later succeed with general populaces. Pornographers produced an adult movie two years after the first publicly screened film in 1895. It is generally acknowledged that the adult entertainment business was the first to make money off the Internet and was among the first to widely exploit instant cameras, pay-per-view television, VCRs, Internet streaming video, online video flash, credit-card verification sites, online social networking chat rooms, membership-only websites (used by terrorists today), encryption coding, and increased file-sharing speed. Most recently, the adult industry found ways to stream videos directly onto the newest popular tablet computers, and it is looking at ways to capitalize on the newest three-dimensional film developments.[cxv]

Texas A&M University history and technology professor Jonathan Coopersmith explains, "It's not necessarily that the porn industry comes up with the ideas, but there's a huge difference in any technology between the idea and the successful application...[the porn industries are] kind of

---

[16] I do not suggest that anyone watch or be involved with pornography. Rather, popular and respected business and marketing journals often publish articles referencing adult entertainment's technological advancements. These articles—discussing trends—will suffice to inform methods to amplify counter-al-Qa`ida voices.

like shock troops, and one of the nice things for them is that they can claim, 'Hey, I'm advancing technology.'"[cxvi]

Pornography is a bellwether for technology and communications progress and one place to look to get out ahead of al-Qa`ida's digital marketing advancements.

16. LEGALITY & MORALITY

What are the legal and moral ramifications of narrative amplification?

On moral grounds, the executor of this book's strategy must understand that marketing a person or group's voice may put that person or group into greater danger. A message that reaches a wider audience will become a greater threat to al-Qa`ida. Al-Qa`ida often targets and kills its threats. In short, be wary that conducting this book's strategy will put people in danger and possibly indirectly cause the death of someone who opposes al-Qa`ida.

However, this important moral consideration must be balanced with two factors.

First, these anti-al-Qa`ida authors already made the risky decision to disseminate their words. This book's strategy calls simply for amplification of narratives that not only already exist but also are already "out there." These narratives may not currently enjoy a lot of media play, but in order to be found in the first place, they are already published on a website, in a newspaper, on the radio, or in a video. Although amplification increases the danger to the lives and livelihoods of counter-extremist authors and their families, these persons already made the decision to take the first step to speak out or write against al-Qa`ida.

Second, if violent extremists target or kill the person or group speaking out against al-Qa`ida, then the anti-al-Qa`ida message is likely to receive even more media and an even greater audience—further amplifying the competing narrative. The person may even earn martyrdom status, and his message will achieve a super-viral effect much like al-Qa`ida's dead ideologues have achieved in violent extremist circles.

On legal grounds, the executor of this book's strategy can stand on two factors.

First, it would be rare that an international copyright law would be broken. Most counter narratives are already disseminated—free and open to the public. In addition, properly citing the source in no way weakens the campaign described in this book. In fact, proper citation and explanation of the authors' credentials is an essential part of selling the message. If the target text is copyrighted and cannot be "copied and pasted" to the world, then the executor of the plan must make the informed decision whether a copyright law is more or less important than ending one of the most violent threats to the West and Islam. Furthermore, a lawsuit may bring controversy and publicity—providing greater readership of the narrative.

Second, amplifying a narrative and putting the narrator in danger is akin to a media story putting someone in the limelight. Although journalistic standards should never inform societal morality, reporting has helped to establish a legal standard. And unlike news stories that conduct investigations to uncover information—previously unknown—about a subject, the plan in this book only amplifies stories that are already modestly disseminated. The identification process in this book does not require original source investigation.

The strategy in this book has moral and legal implications which must be considered before and during a media campaign. However, a successful messaging operation may outweigh legal and moral concerns. The fight against al-Qa`ida is deadly. And in battle—on the Internet or in the desert—a decision must be made on how far one is willing to go to destroy a threat.

17. IMPLEMENTATION

An organization—whether run covertly by the U.S. or another government or run by independent entities—would have the following roles (if using the basic strategy of identify → translate → market). The key is for the organization to be nimble enough to exploit success.

The following describe the roles, more specifically, for a counter-al-Qa`ida messaging campaign:

Chief Executive Officer - Responsible for all operations and personnel.

Operations Officer - Directs and is responsible for the identification, translation, and marketing of counter-violence messages.

Historian - Writes books or articles on operations, successes, and failures for future generations who may face similar threats of extremism. Conducts interviews of all team members as original sources for future historians and researchers.

Attorneys - Advise Operations and Executive Officers on legality of all operations.

Hiring Officers - Solicit applications for linguists. Schedule and conduct interviews to determine ability and suitability.

Accounting Officers - Appropriate money for IT support, web designers, translation tools, and administrative items as needed. Meet Executive Officer's expected future needs.

Film Producers, Directors, and Editors - Continuously create films from already available media and online material to generate emotional responses. Continuously improve films for reposting by web designers.

Web Designers - Create, continuously improve, secure, and maintain a set of anonymous websites and mirror/sister sites using anonymous servers.

Linguists - In the long run, an in-house translation team may be less expensive than outsourcing translations. Translate/interpret from English to other languages and vice versa. Edit/quality control others' translations.

Message Writers - Identify quotes, book sections, and article excerpts from independent counterextremist messages to further disseminate. Draft accurate and unbiased statements of legitimacy and independence of messengers.

Researchers - Find and recommend potentially influential counter-extremism messages in Arab press, Muslim media, online commentary, extremist reactions, and popular media. Triage messages for the message writers.

Metrics Researchers - Measure success of counter-violence messages that the organization issues.

Religion Advisor - Because of his study of and familiarity with Islamic texts, he can check the veracity and potential effectiveness of messages that the organization may identify for translation and dissemination. Trains employees to better identify potential messages that have religious weight. Advises Chief Executive Officer, Linguists, Researchers, and Message Writers.

18. SUCCESS METRICS

With any policy proposal, it is necessary to measure success as the strategy is being implemented. If a message does not appear to be gaining traction online or in the real world, or if a message lacks resonance—meaning it is not independently picked up by mirror websites and echoed in news articles and sermons—the person or team implementing the strategy may wish to abandon that message. Or at least the "amplifiers" may wish to refrain from investing more time and money in that message.

On the flipside, if a message shows the ability to resonate, then the person or organization executing the plan may wish to invest more time and money into creating more sites and conducting more translations of it.

The following are calculable measurements that could be used to see how identified, translated, and disseminated messages resound and reverberate in Muslim communities:

- Numbers of website views.

- Rise in website views daily, weekly, monthly, annually; number of return visits, duration of visits.

- Placement on Google using specified,

agreed-upon search terms.

- Shares via social media (e.g. Twitter, Facebook).

- Number of sites that link back to website.

- Rise in comments/ user feedback on website daily, weekly, monthly, annually.

- Quality of blog comments.

- Time al-Qa`ida leadership spend on taped and videoed messages defending against criticisms on website compared with past al-Qa`ida statements.

- Changes in polls of global support for al-Qa`ida and affiliates citing themes on website.

- Major media network (CNN, FOX, MSNBC, Al Jazeera, Al Arabiyya) time spent on website and/or messages translated on the website.

- Counter-extremism organizations and imams stating they use the website and/or wishing to contribute daily, weekly, monthly, annually.

However, when starting a campaign, one should steal a page out of al-Qa`ida's playbook. Just as al-Qa`ida and affiliates produce sometimes dozens of messages in a week—sometimes slightly contradictory and some narratives a bit off mes-sage—a counter-al-Qa`ida campaign should likewise avoid timidity. If there is doubt whether or not to use a message, use it.

Just as many al-Qa`ida messages come out flat—such as Zawahiri's message criticizing Presi-dent Obama in January 2009 at the top of the President's worldwide popularity—some anti-violent-extremism messages will lack effect. But even weak messages or contradictory messages may force al-Qa`ida to react, wasting its times and giving undue attention to the message in question.

Finally, it is important to understand and accept that all of the above metrics are only indi-cators of success. Even with poll data and interviews, there is no way to get into someone's head to understand exactly how a message has affected him or her. Therefore we can only meas-ure how messages echo in media and communities, how al-Qa`ida reacts, and finally how al-Qa`ida suffers from a new dearth of re-cruits and supporters.

19. OTHER COUNTER-NARRATIVE EFFORTS

There is currently no effective counter-ideology campaign against al-Qa`ida. Although foreign governments, independent groups, and individuals attempt modest and localized counter-marketing, there is little global effect thus far. This is clearly evidenced during online searches, which yield infinitesimal counter-violence messages in a few languages compared with al-Qa`ida's robust, reinforced, and redundant network of easily accessible online narratives and films in multiple languages and on numerous media platforms. Saudi Arabia, Indonesia, and several other countries' governments conduct some online messaging—but only in their languages targeting their citizens.[cxvii] And government affiliation undermines message impact.

A few U.S. private citizens attempt to shut down websites. However, this effort is ineffective, as I explained. It takes minutes for an extremist website creator to bring the site back up under a foreign and/or anonymous host.

The following are a few examples of online efforts to counter al-Qa`ida propaganda. But unfortunately, in all cases the three pillars in this book's proposal (identify, translate, and amplify credentialed voices) are not heeded. First, the campaigns often do not use those persons that have the greatest potential to dissuade would-be extremists such as former militants, relatively independent religious leaders, and terrorist attack victims. Second, the campaigns provide narratives in only a limited number of languages. So, messages will by definition have limited reach. And third, no concerted marketing strategy is apparent.

I will not mention efforts that attempt to somehow "Westernize" Islam, a religion and way of life without borders. And I will not mention programs which appear only to seek government contracts to run seminars "warning" of undefined inherent dangers in Islam. To even mention these organizations' names would be to give them undeserved attention.

P4Peace

In 2009, Singapore's Terrorism Research Centre, which directed a national rehabilitation program, launched the web portal www.P4Peace.com as a source of English-language information on counterterrorism. The website also claims to promote discussion on peaceful alternatives to violent extremism and to instigate a movement to spread competing narratives online.

The site aims to "bring together the brightest minds in counter-terrorism, to share past successes as well as failures, and to help fill up the gaps in knowledge regarding the ideological struggle between terrorist outfits and ourselves."

The website shares summaries and links to think tank and journal articles on al-Qa`ida ideology and counter-narrative analysis to include academic analyses on recanted terrorists and de-radicalization programs.

The site also shares links to institutes that claim to promote peace and a "moderate version" of Islam. Examples are the Quilliam Foundation, United States Institute for Peace, The International Centre for Islam and Pluralism, and Jerusalem Peacemakers.

However, despite the site's claims to promote counter narratives, the website holds no convincing messages from independent sources. It fails to present the type of dynamic, original, and appealing sound bites and multimedia found on an al-Qa`ida recruitment site. On a website tracking service, P4Peace.com had no data[cxviii]—indicating infinitesimal viewership and the absence of any concerted marketing plan.

P4peace.com also suffers from the veneer of Singaporean government influence—further undermining street credibility and any perception of independence.

Al-Sakina

Saudi Arabia launched the al-Sakina online campaign in an attempt to combat online radicalization. Its English and Arabic websites offer religious arguments and rulings against violent threats to the Saudi regime, and a sister online library site offers limited counter narratives just in Arabic. Also, staff roam blogs and websites in an attempt to identify violent extremists and those susceptible to al-Qa`ida or any other anti-regime groups' propaganda.

The Saudi government claims successes on preventing online radicalization as well as de-radicalizing individuals through one-on-one communication with an al-Sakina staff member. However, there is no independent verification or study on the success of the al-Sakina campaign.

Al-Sakina campaign—although it likely has some effect on curbing al-Qa`ida influence in Saudi Arabia—fails to de-legitimize al-Qa`ida, put al-Qa`ida leaders or ideologues on the defensive, or inspire communities to actively check al-Qa`ida growth.

First, bona fides of the majority of messages on its websites are compromised by government influence. The entire effort is openly supported and funded through Saudi Arabia's Ministry of Islamic Affairs.

Second, most of the statements are devoid of the argument streams mentioned in this book. Many messages are just focused on an understanding that only Saudi leadership can ordain violence as permissible at any particular time. This argument is unlikely to persuade many would-be terrorists, especially those already distrustful of the Saudi regime and its economic and security partnerships with some Western countries.

Third, the messages are in Arabic and English, and remain in their original intellectually inaccessible form. In other words, the narratives lack the sound bites, quotable stand-alone passages, short digestible vignettes, small separable chapters, and mass appeal that al-Qa`ida cultivates.

One of the most convincing pieces of evidence of lack of impact is that al-Qa`ida senior leaders have not reacted to al-Sakina campaign's efforts, like they did overwhelmingly following Dr. Fadl's first recantation book in 2007. Al-Qa`ida may make general statements criticizing Saudi's government and clergy (as al-Qa`ida in the Arabian Peninsula has done on average two times per month in 2009 and thus far in 2010 from their safe havens in eastern Yemen), but it does not feel it has to defend against al-Sakina's messages or efforts.

NoTerror.info

NoTerror.info is an Arabic and English counterterrorism site comprising anti-terrorism videos and messages. Its mission is:

> [T]o expose the fallacy of the distorted and politicized teachings used by ungodly extremists to sanctify and justify terrorism. It has become crucial to inform the Muslim and Arab people—particularly the Iraqi people—about the deceptions terrorists employ in distorting the peaceful teachings of Islam. These terrorists, who claim to follow the Islamic Faith, are in truth drowning in an abyss of mistaken beliefs.

> All religions, human codes and ethics, and even our most primitive intuition regard terrorism to be villainous. True Islam also rejects and condemns terrorism. 'Terrorism has no religion' is our on-going communication campaign against extremist ideology that breeds terrorism, and we use Quranic Verses in their true Islamic meaning; free of

the distortion committed by the misguided malicious terrorist.

Terrorists use various means to justify their violence, even though God's written word does not permit these actions. One glance at the victims of terrorist attacks is living proof that terrorists are nothing but criminals and murderers, and are far from being righteous.

Don't the terrorists understand the consequences of their actions? In almost every house in Iraq, mothers are put to loss and children are orphaned through their widespread and merciless killings. They are making the lives of those they claim to be defending the cheapest.

Even the word 'war' does not justify attacking secure civilians and turning the streets into a heinous scene that is open for the slaughter of both innocent women and children. The ethics of war—any war—refute this mass elimination, and we have, in the form of the Prophet, a decent example to follow.

The website has 21 anti-terrorism fictional video vignettes, which can be played in high or low resolution. The videos are also available on Youtube with between 1,712 to 6,094 views on 17 December 2009. As a comparison, violent extremist English-language lecturer Anwar al-Awlaki enjoys as many as 26,518 viewers on his Youtube videos.

The themes themselves are potentially powerful, but the words lack the weight of messages from legitimate, credentialed, and independent voices. Furthermore, the anonymity of the website, according to some, may lead the cynical to assume that the site is run by a government-paid or influenced office.

The professional-looking, well-acted, and slickly edited videos with special effects and emotional music are entertaining and have the potential to draw a large viewership, but it appears that usership is relatively low. According to a free website tracking service, NoTerror.info began May 2006 and has no available traffic rank statistics, user demographic information, or clickstream data—likely indicating relatively low viewership and probably a result of a failure to implement a concerted marketing plan.

Minhaj-ul-Quran International

Dr. Qadri founded the Minhaj-ul-Quran International, located in Lahore, Pakistan, in 1981 as a nonpolitical, non-sectarian, nongovernmental organization reportedly to propagate constructionist Islamic ideas in the interest of peace and open dialogue with other belief systems.

The organization—with many websites to amplify its ideas—wants to be a worldwide movement:

> *The primary aim of the Minhaj-ul-Quran International is to bring about a comprehensive and multidimensional change in society...and revive, once again,*

> *the exterminated moral and spiritual values of Islam...*

The group's explicit goal of a renaissance of ancient practices of Islam is met with a view towards peace and counter-violence. This is seen in the over 600,000 Urdu texts on its many websites—some translated into English and Arabic. The texts often focus on piety, sincerity of faith, universalism, and changing society to be more compassionate and peaceful. Most notable is Dr. Qadri's most recent judgment on the complete impermissibility and "evil" of suicide terrorism.

Along with its main minhaj.org website, the organization has a total of 20 interlinked websites with statements and texts in multiple media platforms.[cxix]

However, three factors keep the group's messages from even competing with al-Qa`ida online efforts.

First, many of the published papers are steeped in rich religious language and sophisticated religious textual references without any concerted effort to market pithy and emotive sound bites and quotations.

Second, statements are stuck in Urdu and sometimes Arabic and English. This translation effort pales in comparison to al-Qa`ida marketing which ensures themes are understood from the Philippines to Trinidad and Tobago.

Third, the websites are riddled with copyright and proprietary warnings. This wall around online intellectual property may keep the messages at bay. A truly universal marketing campaign that would have even a chance at competing with or overtaking al-Qaʿida marketing would allow openly for "copying and pasting" of excerpts with or without proper citation. Al-Qaʿida even openly promotes plagiarism to help propagate its ideas. Counter-al-Qaʿida campaigns would be wise to learn from al-Qaʿida's marketing excellence and dispense with copyrighting for the goal of undermining the most violent and real threat to Islam in the modern age.

20. CONCLUSION

I fear that the advice in this book will go unheeded at first. I fear that senior field commanders and politicians will continue to judge war success by enemies captured worldwide and villages under local government control in Iraq and Afghanistan. I fear that many more attacks and many more deaths will be necessary for al-Qa`ida to defeat itself—for populations to completely starve al-Qa`ida of any semblance of support.

But this need not be the case. We must understand that al-Qa`ida media is not a side-show and not a supporting effort—it is its everything. Without its media it would not grow. It would not be relevant. It would not be a continual threat to the United States.

Once enough leaders of al-Qa`ida are six feet under and once we see that this has failed to alter the enemy, I trust that U.S. leadership will realize that more needs to be done to undermine al-Qa`ida's regenerative nature.

My plan is one route. It is a roadmap for speeding al-Qa`ida's self-destruction—to lessen the time it will take for the group's own inevitable demise. And this plan can and must become a blueprint for defeating all violent transnational insurrections: inspire revolt through exposure of the organization's own violent ideology; radicalize the would-be victims against the threat before they become victims.

Driven to defend Islam against the West with romantic dreams of a heroic, David-and-Goliath-like fight that will end in paradise, al-Qaʿida's following will continue to grow as it stands now. However, effective counter-messaging will drive a permanent schism between mainstream Muslims and al-Qaʿida. Although experts in intelligence, security, and academia agree on the centrality of winning the "war of ideas," there is currently no concerted information plan in place to slow the spread of violent ideology. A determined counter-messaging effort must start immediately. Otherwise, the West and Islam will continue to spend untold sums and lives fighting these terrorists one at a time for decades, maybe centuries, to come.

The fire that currently drives young Muslims to fight and die should be turned against al-Qaʿida. Once radical leaders are ideologically isolated, recruitment pools will diminish. The active and passive support of Muslims, on which al-Qaʿida and its affiliates rely, will die.

The war against al-Qaʿida is a war for the hearts and minds of Muslims. It is a struggle within Islam. A strategy to empower Muslims and Muslim voices will defeat al-Qaʿida.

BIBLIOGRAPHY

Primary Sources

Abas, Nasir, *Membongkar Jamaah Islamiyah: Pengakuan Mantan Anggota JI* (Unveiling Jamaah Islamiyah: Confessions of an Ex-JI Member), Jakarta: Grafindo Khazanah Ilmu, 2005.

al-Awdah, Salman, "A Ramadan Letter to Usama bin Ladin," *Muslim Matters*, http://muslimmatters.org/2007/09/18/shaykh-salman-al-oudahs-ramadan-letter-to-Usama-bin-Ladin-on-nbc/, 2007.

al-Awdah, Salman, "We Must be Unequivocal in Condemning Violence," *Islam Today*, http://www.islamtoday.com/showme_weekly_2006.cfm?cat_id=30&sub_cat_id=1134, 2006.

al-Awlaki, Anwar, "Constants of Jihad," 2006.

Center for Moderate Muslim Indonesia on Radio Republic Indonesia, "Nasir Abas on Jamaah Islamiyah," *Indonesia Matters*, http://www.indonesiamatters.com/104/nasir-abas-on-jamaah-islamiyah/, February 2006.

Faraj, Muhammad, *Abd al-Salam, Al-Faridah al-Gha'ibah* (The Neglected Duty), translated by Johanned J. G. Jansen, New York: MacMillan Publishing Company, 1986.

El Fazazi, Mohammed, "Letter: Germany is No Battle Zone," *Professional Soldiers*, http://www.professionalsoldiers.com/forums/showthread.php?p=292319, July 2009.

Jaafar, Muhammad Abu,"Salafist Protectors against Bombings Afflicting Muslims in Algeria," http://dhdsdz.blogspot.com/2008/01/blog-post_3547.html, 2008.

Ladin, Usama bin, Audio/Video/Written Statements and interviews from 1999–today, The NEFA Foundation, http://www1.nefafoundation.org:80/documents-aqstatements.html.

Libyan Islamic Fighting Group Leadership, "A Selected Translation of the LIFG Recantation Document," translated by Mohammed Ali Musawi, Quilliam Foundation, http://quilliamfoundation.org/images/a_selected_translation_of_the_lifg.pdf , October 2009.

Qutb, Sayyid, *Ma'alim fi-l-Tariq* (Milestones), Damascus: Dar al-Ilm, 1964.

Rehman, Grand Mufti Habibur, "Fatwa Against Terrorism" (in English), *Madrasa Reforms in India*, http://madrasareforms. blogspot.com/2008/06/text-of-darul-uloom-deobands-fatwa.html, February 2008.

al-Sharif, Sayyid Imam, Exposure of the Exoneration Book (in 13 episodes), *Al-Masry Al-Yawm* daily newspaper, November–December 2008.

al-Sharif, Sayyid Imam, *Foundations for the Preparation of Jihad*, 1988.

al-Sharif, Sayyid Imam, *Wathiqat Tarshid Al-'Aml Al-Jihadi fi Misr w'Al-'Alam* (Advice Regarding the Conduct of Jihadist Action in Egypt and the World), Aljareeda.com in chapters, 19 November 2007–5 December 2007.

al-Zawahiri, Ayman, Audio/Video/Written Statements and interviews from 1999–today, The NEFA Foundation, http://www1.nefafoundation.org:80/documents-aqstatements.html.

al-Zawahiri, Ayman, "The Exoneration: A Treatise Exonerating the Community of the Pen and the Sword from the Debilitating Accusation of Fatigue and Weakness," Ekhlas web forum, 2008.

al-Zawahiri, Ayman, "Knights Under the Prophet's Banner," Serialized in *Al-Sharq al-Awsat* (London, December 2, 2001) from Sageman, Marc, *Understanding Terror Networks*, Philadelphia: University of Pennsylvania Press, 2004.

al-Zayyat, Montasser, *The Road to al-Qaeda: The Story of Bin Ladin's Right-Hand Man*, translated by Ahmed Fekry, London; Sterling, Virginia: Pluto Press, 2004.

Surveys & Polls (and Studies Comprising Surveys & Polls)

Bakker, Dr. Edwin, "Jihadi Terrorists in Europe," Netherlands Institute of International Relations, 2006.

Berko, Anat, "The Path to Paradise: The Inner World of Suicide Bombers and Their Dispatchers," Praeger Security International, 2007.

Cardash, Sharon; Cillufo, Frank; Lane, Jan; Saathoff, Gregory; Whitehead, Andrew, "Networked Radicalization: A Counter-Strategy," The George Washington University Homeland Security Policy Institute & the University of Virginia Critical Analysis Group, 2006.

Combating Terrorism Center, West Point, "The Militant Ideology Atlas Executive Report," November 2006.

The International Centre for the Study of Radicalisation and Political Violence, "Countering Online Radicalisation: A Strategy for Action," www.icsr.info, 2009.

The International Centre for the Study of Radicalisation and Political Violence, "Prisons and Terrorism: Radicalisation and De-radicalisation in 15 Countries," www.icsr.info, 2010.

Pape, Robert, "Dying to Win: The Strategic Logic of Suicide Terrorism," New York: Random House, 2006.

Pew Research Center, "Global Opinion Trends 2002-2007: A Rising Tide Lifts Mood in the Developing World," http://pewglobal.org/reports/display.php?ReportID=257, 2007.

Pew Research Center Global Attitudes Project, "22-Nation Pew Global Attitudes Survey," 17 June 2010.

Sageman, Marc, *Understanding Terror Networks*, Philadelphia: University of Pennsylvania Press, 2004.

United Nations Assistance Mission to Afghanistan, "Suicide Attacks in Afghanistan (2001-2007)," 2007.

Literature

Atwan, Abdel Bari, *The Secret History of al Qaeda*, Berkeley: University of California Press, 2006.

Bergen, Peter; Cruickshank, Paul, "The Unraveling: The Jihadist Revolt Against bin Ladin," *The New Republic*, http://www.tnr.com/article/the-unraveling, 11 June 2008.

Black, Andrew, "The Ideological Struggle Over al-Qaeda's Suicide Tactics in Algeria," *Terrorism Monitor* Volume 6, Issue 3, 7 February 2008.

Blakely, Rhys, "Darool-Uloom Deoband Issues Fatwa against Terrorism," *Times Online*, http://www.timesonline.co.uk/tol/news/world/asia/article4045862.ece, 2 June 2008.

Boucek, Christopher, "Extremism Reeducation and Rehabilitation in Saudi Arabia," *Terrorism Monitor*, The Jamestown Foundation, Volume V, Issue 16, 16 August 2007.

Boucek, Christopher, "Yemen: Avoiding a Downward Spiral," Carnegie Endowment for International Peace, September 2009.

Brachman, Jarret, "Abu Yahya's Six Easy Steps for Defeating al-Qaeda," *Perspectives on Terrorism*, Volume I Issue 5, http://www.terrorismanalysts.com/pt/index.php?option=com_rokzine&view=article&id=18&Itemid=54, 2007.

Byman, Daniel, "Taliban vs. Predator," *Foreign Affairs*, March/April 2009.

Clark, Howard, *How You Can Kill Al-Qaeda*, New Orleans: Light of New Orleans, 2009.

Cleveland, William, *A History of the Modern Middle East*, Oxford: Westview Press, 1994.

Day, Stephen, "Updating Yemeni National Unity," *The Middle East Journal*, Volume 62, Number 3, Summer 2008.

Esposito, John L., *Unholy War: Terror in the Name of Islam*, Oxford: Oxford University Press, 2002.

Fuller, Graham, *The Future of Political Islam*, New York: Palgrave MacMillan, 2003.

Gerges, Fawaz, *Journey of the Jihadist: Inside Muslim Militancy*, London: Harcourt, 2007.

Kepel, Gilles, *Jihad: The Trail of Political Islam*, translated by Anthony F. Roberts, Cambridge: Harvard University Press, 2002.

Kepel, Gilles, *Muslim Extremism in Egypt: The Prophet and Pharaoh*, translated by Jon Rothschild, Berkeley: University of California Press, 2003.

Kepel, Gilles, *The Roots of Radical Islam*, translated by Jon Rothchild, London: Saqi, 2005.

Haddad, Yvonne Y., "Sayyid Qutb: Ideologue of Islamic Revival," in John L. Esposito (ed.), *Voices of Resurgent Islam*, Oxford: Oxford University Press, 1983.

Hallaq, Wael B., *Shari`a*, Cambridge: Cambridge University Press, 2009.

Hill, Ginny, "Yemen: Fear of Failure," Chatham House, November 2008.

Hoffman, Dr. Bruce, *Inside Terrorism*, New York: Columbia University Press, 2006.

Hoffman, Dr. Bruce, "The Use of the Internet by Islamic Extremists," Statement before the U.S. House of Representatives Permanent Select Committee on Intelligence, 4 May 2006.

Horgan, John; Bjorge, Tore (Editors), *Leaving Terrorism Behind: Individual and Collective Disengagement*, London: Routledge, 2009.

Horgan, John, *Walking Away From Terrorism: Accounts of Disengagement from Radical and Extremist Movements*, London: Routledge, 2009.

Hudson, Rex, *Who Becomes a Terrorist and Why: The 1999 Government Report on Profiling Terrorists*, Connecticut: The Lyons Press, 1999.

Jones, Seth; Libicki, Martin, *How Terrorist Groups End: Lessons for Countering al Qa`ida*, Santa Monica, RAND, 2008.

Killcullen, David, *The Accidental Guerrilla: Fighting Small Wars in the Midst of a Big One*, Oxford: Oxford University Press, 2009.

Lynch, Marc, "Al-Qaeda's Media Strategies," *The National Interest Online*, http://www.nationalinterest.org/Article.aspx?id=11524, 1 March 2006.

Malik, Shiv, "My Brother the Bomber," *Prospect*, http://www.prospectmagazine.co.uk/article_details.php?id=9635, June 2007.

An-Na`im, Abdullahi Ahmed, *Islam and the Secular State*, Cambridge: Harvard University Press, 2008.

National Coordinator for Counterterrorism, "Jihadis and the Internet," Netherlands Ministries of Justice and of the Interior and Kingdom Relations, www.investigativeproject.org/documents/testimony/226.pdf, February 2007.

Nawaz, Shuja, "FATA—A Most Dangerous Place," CSIS, January 2009.

Rapoport, David C., The Four Waves of Modern Terrorism, http://www.isop.ucla.edu/article.asp?parentid=47153, 5 June 2006.

Wright, Lawrence, *The Looming Tower: Al-Qaeda and the Road to 9/11*, New York: Random House, 2006.

Wright, Lawrence, "The Rebellion Within: An Al Qaeda Mastermind Questions Terrorism," *The New Yorker,* http://www.newyorker.com/reporting/2008/06/02/080602fa _fact_wright, 2 June 2008.

ENDNOTES

[i] *New York Times*, "7 Months, 10 Days in Captivity," 18 October 2009, http://www.nytimes.com/2009/10/18/world/asia/18hostage.html.

[ii] Lieutenant General William P. Yarborough, *Counter Insurgency Operations*, 1962.

[iii] *Washington Post*, "U.S. Training Afghan Villagers to Fight the Taliban," 27 April 2010.

[iv] *Washington Post*, "U.S. Training Afghan Villagers to Fight the Taliban," 27 April 2010.

[v] Robert Haddick, "This Week at War: Do We Still Need Special Ops?" *Foreign Policy*, 23 April 2010.

[vi] *U.S. Special Operations Command Strategy 2010*, 1 November 2009 (unclassified).

[vii] *Washington Post*, "U.S. eager to replicate Afghan villagers' successful revolt against Taliban," http://www.washingtonpost.com/wp-dyn/content/article/2010/06/20/AR2010062003479.html, 21 June 2010.

[viii] *New York Times*, "Munich Imam Tries to Dull Lure of Radical Islam," 16 May 2010.

[ix] Pew Research Center, "Global Opinion Trends 2002-2007: A Rising Tide Lifts Mood in the Developing World," 2007.

[x] *Boston Globe*, "Jihad: A Global Fad," 1 August 2006.

[xi] Sharon Cardash, Frank Cillufo, Jan Lane, Gregory Saathoff, Andrew Whitehead, "Net-worked Radicalization: A Counter-Strategy," The George Washington University Home-land Security Policy Institute & The University of Virginia Critical Analysis Group, 2006; Dr. Bruce Hoffman, "The Use of the Internet by Islamic Extremists," Statement before the U.S. House of Representatives Permanent Select Committee on Intelligence, 4 May 2006; National Coordinator for Counterterrorism, "Jihadis and the Internet," Nether-lands Ministries of Justice and of the Interior and Kingdom Relations, www.investigativeproject.org/documents/testimony/226.pdf, February 2007; *Washington Post*, "Al-Qa`ida's Growing Online Offensive," http://www.washingtonpost.com/wp-dyn/content/article/2008/06/23/AR2008062302135.html, 24 June 2008.

[xii] *Guardian.co.uk*, "The Making of an Extremist," 20 August 2008.

[xiii] Sharon Cardash, Frank Cillufo, Jan Lane, Gregory Saathoff, Andrew Whitehead, "Networked Radicalization: A Counter-Strategy," The George Washington University Homeland Security Policy Institute & The University of Virginia Critical Analysis Group, 2006.

[xiv] *New York Times*, "An Internet Jihad Aims at U.S. Viewers," http://www.nytimes.com/2007/10/15/us/15net.html?_r=2&ref=world, 15 October 2007. *The National Interest Online*, Al-Qa`ida's Media Strategies, http://www.nationalinterest.org/Article.aspx?id=11524, 1 March 2006.

[xv] *Al Mosul Jihad* Magazine, "Defenders of the Truth," July 2009; *Al Mosul Jihad* Magazine, "Defenders of the Truth," August 2009; Ansarnet.info, 16 October 2009; Ansarnet.info, 15 October 2009.

[xvi] *Long War Journal*, Transcript of Adam Gadahn's "A Call To Arms," 8 March 2010, http://www.longwarjournal.org/threat-matrix/archives/2010/03/transcript_of_adam_gadahns_a_c.php.

[xvii] *Timesonline.co.uk*, "Umar Farouk Abdulmutallab: One Boy's Journey to Jihad," 3 January 2010, http://www.timesonline.co.uk/tol/news/world/middle_east/article6974073.ece.

[xviii] United States District Court, District of New Jersey, United States of America versus Mohamad Ibrahim Shnewer, Dritan Duka, Eljkir Duka, Shain Duka, and Serdar Tatar, Government Exhibit Ciminal Number 07-459, (conversation: 23 February 2007, 7:31 pm). United States District Court, District of New Jersey, United States of America versus Mohamad Ibrahim Shnewer, Dritan Duka, Eljkir Duka, Shain Duka, and Serdar Tatar, Government Exhibit Ciminal Number 07-459, (conversation: 23 February 2007, 9:39 pm).

[xix] Marc Sageman, *Understanding Terror Networks*, Philadelphia: University of Pennsylvania Press, 2004.

[xx] Edwin Bakker, Netherlands Institute of International Relations, *Jihadi Terrorists in Europe*, December 2006.

[xxi] Robert A. Pape, *The Strategic Logic of Suicide Terrorism*, New York: Random House, 2005.

[xxii] Anat Berko (translated by Elizabeth Yuval), *The Path to Paradise: The Inner World of Suicide Bombers and Their Dispatchers*, Praeger Security International, 2007.

[xxiii] Colonel John M. Venhaus, "Why Youth Join al-Qaeda," United States Institute of Peace, May 2010.

[xxiv] Kepel, Gilles, *Jihad: The Trail of Political Islam*, translated by Anthony F. Roberts, Cambridge: Harvard University Press, 2002.

[xxv] Marc Sageman, *Understanding Terror Networks*, Philadelphia: University of Pennsylvania Press, 2004.

xxvi Dr. Israel Elad Altman, "Current Trends in the Ideology of the Egyptian Muslim Brotherhood," in *Current Trends in Islamist Ideology*, Hudson Institute, January 2005.

xxvii Yvonne Y. Haddad, "Sayyid Qutb: Ideologue of Islamic Revival," in John L. Esposito (ed.), *Voices of Resurgent Islam*, Oxford: Oxford University Press, 1983.

xxviii Gilles Kepel, *Muslim Extremism in Egypt: The Prophet and Pharaoh*, translated by Jon Rothschild, Berkeley: University of California Press, 2003.

xxix Ibid.

xxx Sayyid Qutb, *Milestones*, (in English translation), Damascus: Dar al-Ilm, 1964.

xxxi Lawrence Wright, *The Looming Tower: Al-Qa`ida and the Road to 9/11*, New York: Random House, 2006.

xxxii Marc Sageman, *Understanding Terror Networks*, Philadelphia: University of Pennsylvania Press, 2004.

xxxiii Rudolf Peters, "The Political Relevance of the Doctrine of Jihad in Sadat's Egypt", chapter 14 in *National and International Politics in the Middle East: Essays in Honour of Elie Kedourie*, edited by Edward Ingram, London: Routledge, 2004.

xxxiv Gilles Kepel, *Muslim Extremism in Egypt: The Prophet and Pharaoh*, translated by Jon Rothschild, Berkeley: University of California Press, 2003.

xxxv Ibid.

xxxvi Ibid.

xxxvii Muhammad 'Abd al-Salam Faraj, *The Neglected Duty* (The Creed of Sadat's Assassins and Islamic Resurgence in the Middle East), translated by Johanned J. G. Jansen, New York: MacMillan Publishing Company, 1986.

xxxviii Gilles Kepel, *Muslim Extremism in Egypt: The Prophet and Pharaoh*, translated by Jon Rothschild, Berkeley: University of California Press, 2003.

xxxix Muhammad 'Abd al-Salam Faraj, *The Neglected Duty* (The Creed of Sadat's Assassins and Islamic Resurgence in the Middle East), translated by Johanned J. G. Jansen, New York: MacMillan Publishing Company, 1986.

xl Ibid.

xli Ibid.

xlii Ibid.

xliii Thomas W. Lippman, *Egypt After Nasser: Sadat, Peace and the Mirage of Prosperity*, New York: Paragon House, 1989.

xliv Montasser Al-Zayyat, *The Road to Al-Qa`ida: The Story of Bin Ladin's Right Hand Man*, translated by Ahmed Fekry, London; Sterling, Virginia: Pluto Press, 2004.

[xlv] *The Guardian*, "UK Source in Egypt Reports on Jailed Terrorist Leader's Renunciation of Violence," 27 July 2007.

[xlvi] Combating Terrorism Center, West Point, *The Militant Ideology Atlas Executive Report*, November, 2006.

[xlvii] Montasser Al-Zayyat, *The Road to Al-Qa`ida: The Story of Bin Ladin's Right Hand Man*, translated by Ahmed Fekry, London; Sterling, Virginia: Pluto Press, 2004.

[xlviii] Lawrence Wright, *The Looming Tower: Al-Qaeda and the Road to 9/11*, New York: Random House, 2006.

[xlix] Kamil al-Tawil, "The Reviews of the Jihadists' Theorist have been Referred to Al-Azhar," Al Hayat website, 24 June 2007, BBC Monitoring International Reports, 3 July 2007.

[l] Montasser Al-Zayyat, *The Road to Al-Qa`ida: The Story of Bin Ladin's Right Hand Man*, translated by Ahmed Fekry, London; Sterling, Virginia: Pluto Press, 2004.

[li] Lawrence Wright, *The Looming Tower: Al-Qaeda and the Road to 9/11*, New York: Random House, 2006.

[lii] Ibid.

[liii] Lawrence Wright, "My Trip to Al-Qa`ida," Lecture, Washington, DC, 27 September 2007.

[liv] Lawrence Wright, *The Looming Tower: Al-Qaeda and the Road to 9/11*, New York: Random House, 2006.

[lv] Marc Sageman, *Understanding Terror Networks*, Philadelphia: University of Pennsylvania Press, 2004.

[lvi] Ibid.

[lvii] *IslamToday.com*, accessed 14 December 2009, islamtoday.com; NEFA Foundation, 15 November 2009. http://www.nefafoundation.org/miscellaneous/nefa_awdahhasan1109.pdf; Muslimmatters.org, 18 September 2007, http://muslimmatters.org/2007/09/18/shaykh-salman-al-oudahs-ramadan-letter-to-Usama-bin-Ladin-on-nbc/.

[lviii] Alexa.com, accessed 14 December 2009, alexa.com.

[lix] *Spiegel Online*, 29 October 2009, http://www.spiegel.de/international/world/0,1518,658103,00.html; *Spiegel Online*, 30 October 2009, http://www.spiegel.de/international/germany/0,1518,657413,00.html.

[lx] *Jamiat Ulama-i-Hind*, accessed 24 November 2009, http://jamiatulamaihind.org/home.html; Madrasa Reforms in India, 4 June 2008, http://madrasareforms.blogspot.com/2008/06/text-of-darul-uloom-deobands-fatwa.html; *The Independent*, 2 June 2008, http://www.independent.co.uk/news/world/asia/muslim-seminary-issues-fatwa-against-terrorism-838162.html.

[lxi] PBS, 4 January 2010, http://www.pbs.org/newshour/bb/terrorism/jan-june10/yemen_01-04.html; President Saleh's official website, accessed 17 January 2010, http://www.presidentsaleh.gov.ye/

shownews.php?lng=en&_nsid=7946; *YemenPortal.net*, 11 January 2010, http://yemenportal.net/english/index.php?source=yemenpost_eng&me nu=1&start=0; *Yemen Post*, 14 January 2010, http://yemenpost.net/Detail123456789.aspx?ID=3&SubID=1777.
[lxii] *Politiken Daily*, 28 October 2009, http://i.pol.dk/newsinenglish /article819280.ece.
[lxiii] Jamestown Foundation, *Terrorism Monitor* Volume 8 Issue 14, "Controversial Gathering of Islamic Scholars Refutes Al-Qaeda's Ideological Cornerstone," 9 April 2010, http://www.jamestown.org/single/?no_cache=1&tx_ttnews per-cent5Btt_news percent5D=36248&tx_ttnews percent5BbackPid percent5D=228&cHash=18f490beca.
[lxiv] Albar Sheikh identified the following URLs for the author: http://www.foreignpolicy.com/articles/2010/04/14/sheikh_to_terrorist s_go_to_hell?page=full; http://news.bbc.co.uk/2/hi/uk_news/8544531.stm; http://newsweek.washingtonpost.com/onfaith/panelists/john_esposito /2010/03/influential_pakistani_cleric_issues_fatwa_against_terrorism.h tml; http://www.time.com/time/world/article/0,8599,196 9662,00.html; http://news.bbc.co.uk/today/hi/listen_again/newsid _8544000/8544843.stm; http://www.minhaj.org/english/index.html.
[lxv] Ibid.
[lxvi] Lawrence Wright, "The Rebellion Within: An Al Qa'ida Mastermind Questions Terrorism," The New Yorker, http://www.newyorker.com/reporting/2008/06/02/080602fa_fact_wri ght, 2 June 2008; Combating Terrorism Center, West Point, *The Militant Ideology Atlas Executive Report*, November 2006; Peter Bergen and Paul Cruickshank, "The Unraveling: The Jihadist Revolt against bin Ladin," The New Republic, http://www.tnr.com/article/the-unraveling, 11 June 2008; "Exoneration: A Treatise Exonerating the Community of the Pen and the Sword from the Debilitating Accusation of Fatigue and Weakness," 2008.
[lxvii] al-Sharif, Sayyid Imam (Dr. Fadl), "Advice Regarding the Conduct of Jihadist Action in Egypt and the World," Aljareed.com, December 2007.
[lxviii] Gama'a Islamiyya, egyip.com, accessed 14 February 2010.
[lxix] Islamic Group website, accessed 14 December 2009; Alexa.com, accessed 11 December 2009, alexa.com; Muhammad 'Abd al-Salam Faraj, *Al-Faridah al-Gha'ibah (The Neglected Duty)*, translated by Johan-ned J. G. Jansen, New York: MacMillan Publishing Company, 1986; Sayyid Qutb, Ma'alim fi-l-Tariq *(Milestones)*, Damascus: Dar al-Ilm, 1964; William Cleveland, *A History of the Modern Middle East*, Oxford: Westview Press, 1994; John L. Esposito, *Unholy War: Terror in the Name of Islam*, Oxford: Oxford University Press, 2002; Gilles Kepel, *Jihad: The Trail of Political Islam*, translated by Anthony F. Roberts, Cambridge:

Harvard University Press, 2002; Gilles Kepel, *Muslim Extremism in Egypt: The Prophet and Pharaoh*, translated by Jon Rothschild, Berkeley: University of California Press, 2003; Yvonne Y. Haddad, "Sayyid Qutb: Ideologue of Islamic Revival," in John L. Esposito (ed.), *Voices of Resurgent Islam*, Oxford: Oxford University Press, 1983; Lawrence Wright, *The Looming Tower: Al-Qa'ida and the Road to 9/11*, New York: Random House, 2006.

[lxx] *Magharebia* online, 21 January 2009, http://www.magharebia.com/co-coon/awi/xhtml1/en_GB/features/awi/features/2009/01/21/feature-01; *Magharebia* online, 10 February 2009, http://www.magharebia.com/cocoon/awi/xhtml1/en_GB/features/awi/newsbriefs/general/2009/02/10/newsbrief-01.

[lxxi] *Magharebia* online, "Bin Laden's former bodyguard calls on youth to reject violence," 12 May 2010, http://www.magharebia.com.

[lxxii] *Ibid.*

[lxxiii] *BBC*, 12 November 2009, http://news.bbc.co.uk/2/hi/south_asia/8357011.stm; *Washington Times*, 2 July 2009, http://www.washingtontimes.com/news/2009/jul/02/taliban-buying-children-to-serve-as-suicide-bomber/; *PBS*, 14 April 2009, http://www.pbs.org/frontlineworld/stories/pakistan802/; *Long War Journal*, 6 October 2008, http://www.longwarjournal.org/archives/2008/10/taliban_rebuild_chil.php; U.N. News Centre, 19 January 2009, http://www.un.org/apps/news/story.asp?NewsID=29589&Cr=taliban&Cr1=children; *CNN*, 7 July 2009, http://www.cnn.com/2009/WORLD/asiapcf/07/07/pakistan.child.bombers/index.html.

[lxxiv] *BBC*, 4 February 2010, http://news.bbc.co.uk/2/hi/south_asia/8499615.stm.

[lxxv] *Al Arabiya*, accessed 25 February 2010, http://www.alarabiya.net.

[lxxvi] *BBC.com*, 10 December 2009, http://news.bbc.co.uk/2/hi/middle_east/8405235.stm; *Associated Press*, 15 October 2009; *Al Qimmah*, 13 November 2009, http://www.alqimmah.net/showthread.php?p=22862; Islamic Awakening, 13 November 2009, http://forums.islamicawakening.com/f18/top-al-qaeda-leader-blames-blackwater-peshawar-blasts-30199/.

lxxvii Pew Research Center Global Attitudes Project, "22-Nation Pew Global Attitudes Survey," 17 June 2010.

[lxxviii] Combating Terrorism Center, West Point, *The Militant Ideology Atlas Executive Report*, November, 2006.

[lxxix] *Ibid.*

[lxxx] Daniel W. Brown, *Rethinking Tradition in Modern Islamic Thought*, Cambridge: Cambridge University Press, 1996; G. H. A. Juynboll, *The Authenticity of the Tradition Literature: Discussions in Modern Egypt*, Leiden: Brill, 1969; *Combating Terrorism Center Sentinel*, May 2008,

http://www.ctc.usma.edu/sentinel/CTCSentinel-Vol1Iss6.pdf; American Enterprise Institute, September 2008,
http://www.aei.org/outlook/28598.

[lxxi] John L. Esposito, *Unholy War: Terror in the Name of Islam*, Oxford: Oxford University Press, 2002.

[lxxii] Dr. Muhammad Tahir-ul-Qadri, *Introduction to the Fatwa on Suicide Bombings and Terrorism*, translated by Shaykh Abdul Aziz Dabbagh, Mihaj-ul-Quran International, Februrary 2010.

[lxxiii] Ayman al-Zawahiri, Audio/Video/Written Statements and interviews from 1999–today, http://www1.nefafoundation.org:80/documents-aqstatements.html; Usama bin Ladin, Audio/Video/Written Statements and interviews from 1999 – today, http://www1.nefafoundation.org:80/documents-aqstatements.html.

[lxxiv] Jarret Brachman, "Abu Yahya's Six Easy Steps for Defeating al-Qaeda," *Perspectives on Terrorism*, Volume I Issue 5,
http://www.terrorismanalysts.com/pt/index.php?option=com_rokzine&view=article&id=18&Itemid=54, 2007.

[lxxv] David C. Rapoport, "The Four Waves of Modern Terrorism," UCLA International Institute, http://www.isop.ucla.edu/article.asp?parentid=47153, 5 June 2006.

[lxxvi] Anwar al-Alawki, "Constants of Jihad," 2006; http://www.anwar-alawlaki.com/, accessed 10 January 2009.

[lxxvii] Usama bin Ladin, Audio/Video/Written Statements and inter-views from 1999–today, http://www1.nefafoundation.org:80/documents-aqstatements.html.

[lxxviii] Interviews with Marines.

[lxxix] Daniel W. Brown, *Rethinking Tradition in Modern Islamic Thought*, Cambridge: Cambridge University Press, 1996; G. H. A. Juynboll, *The Authenticity of the Tradition Literature: Discussions in Modern Egypt*, Leiden: Brill, 1969; *Combating Terrorism Center Sentinel*, May 2008, http://www.ctc.usma.edu/sentinel/CTCSentinel-Vol1Iss6.pdf; American Enterprise Institute, September 2008,
http://www.aei.org/outlook/28598; Wael B. Hallaq, *Shari`a*, Cambridge: Cambridge University Press, 2009.

[xc] *IRIN*, Yemen: "Unprecedented Water Rationing in Cities," 16 August 2009, http://www.irinnews.org/report.aspx?ReportId=85734.

[xci] *TimesOnline*, "Yemen Could Become First Nation to Run Out of Water," 21 October 2009, http://www.timesonline.co.uk/tol/news/environment/article6883051.ece.

[xcii] *Christian Science Monitor*, "At Heart of Yemen's Conflicts: Water Crisis," 5 November 2009.

[xciii] *LA Times*, "Yemen Water Crisis Builds," 11 October 2009, http://articles.latimes.com/2009/oct/11/world/fg-yemen-water11.

[xciv] *IRIN*, Yemen: "Unprecedented Water Rationing in Cities," 16 August 2009, http://www.irinnews.org/report.aspx?ReportId=85734.

[xlv] *TimesOnline*, "Yemen Could Become First Nation to Run Out of Water," 21 October 2009, http://www.timesonline.co.uk/tol/news/environment/article6883051.ece.

[xcvi] *Christian Science Monitor*, "At Heart of Yemen's Conflicts: Water Crisis," 5 November 2009.

[xcvii] *LA Times*, "Yemen Water Crisis Builds," 11 October 2009, http://articles.latimes.com/2009/oct/11/world/fg-yemen-water11.

[xcviii] *TimesOnline*, "Yemen Could Become First Nation to Run Out of Water," 21 October 2009, http://www.timesonline.co.uk/tol/news/environment/article6883051.ece.

[xcix] *Christian Science Monitor*, "At Heart of Yemen's Conflicts: Water Crisis," 5 November 2009.

[c] *LA Times*, "Yemen Water Crisis Builds," 11 October 2009, http://articles.latimes.com/2009/oct/11/world/fg-yemen-water11.

[ci] *IRIN*, Yemen: "Unprecedented Water Rationing in Cities," 16 August 2009, http://www.irinnews.org/report.aspx?ReportId=85734.

[cii] *The Times*, "Yemen: A Thirsty Nation," 21 October 2009, http://globalpolicy.org/component/content/article/198-natural-resources/48337-yemen-a-thirsty-nation.html.

[ciii] *Christian Science Monitor*, "At Heart of Yemen's Conflicts: Water Crisis," 5 November 2009.

[civ] *LA Times*, "Yemen Water Crisis Builds," 11 October 2009, http://articles.latimes.com/2009/oct/11/world/fg-yemen-water11.

[cv] *The Times*, "Yemen: A Thirsty Nation," 21 October 2009, http://globalpolicy.org/component/content/article/198-natural-resources/48337-yemen-a-thirsty-nation.html.

[cvi] *Christian Science Monitor*, "At Heart of Yemen's Conflicts: Water Crisis," 5 November 2009.

[cvii] *TimesOnline*, "Yemen Could Become First Nation to Run Out of Water," 21 October 2009, http://www.timesonline.co.uk/tol/news/environment/article6883051.ece.

[cviii] *Christian Science Monitor*, "At Heart of Yemen's Conflicts: Water Crisis," 5 November 2009.

[cix] *LA Times*, "Yemen Water Crisis Builds," 11 October 2009, http://articles.latimes.com/2009/oct/11/world/fg-yemen-water11.

[cx] *Washington Times*, "Yemen's Capital Running Out of Water," 15 November 2009, http://www.washingtontimes.com/news/2009/nov/15/yemens-capital-running-out-of-water/.

[cxi] *Prospect Magazine*, "My Brother the Bomber," http://www.prospectmagazine.co.uk/2007/06/mybrotherthebomber/, June 2007.

[cxii] Association for the Advancement of Artificial Intelligence, "Machine Translation," aaai.org, accessed 15 April 2009; Scott Bass, "Machine Vs. Human Translation," Advanced Language Translation Inc., http://www.advancedlanguage.com, 1999; Peter F. Brown, Robert L. Mercer, Stephan A. Della Pietra, Vincent J. Della Pietra, "The Mathematics of Statistical Machine Translation: Parameter Estimation," *Computations Linguistics*, Volume 19 Number 2; Kenneth W. Church, Eduard H. Hovy, "Good applications for crummy machine translation," *Machine Translation Journal*, Volume 8 Number 4, December 1993; Michel Galley, Mark Hopkins, Kevin Knight, Daniel Marcu, "What's in a Translation Rule" DARPA Contract N66001-00-1-9814, Columbia University Department of Computer Science, 2004; Google Inc., "Translate FAQ," www.google.co.uk/help/faq_translation.html, last accessed 18 April 2009; Kevin Heisler, "Google Translate Goes Live with Human Translators," searchenginewatch.com, 4 August 2008; W. John Hutchins, Harold L. Somer, "An Introduction to Machine Translation," Academic Press, Inc., http://www.hutchinsweb.me.uk/IntroMT-0-Contents.pdf, 1992; Nathania Johnson, "Google Enables Cross-Language Search for Enterprise Search Appliance," searchenginewatch.com, 19 December 2008; Nathania Johnson, "Google Explains the Nuances of Language Translation," searchenginewatch.com, 2 January 2009; Nathania Johnson, "Google Translate Adds Widget, Notranslate Code Snippets," searchenginewatch.com, 15 October 2008; Martin Kay, "The Proper Place of Men and Machines in Language Translation," *Machine Translation Journal*, Springer, Netherlands, Volume 12 Numbers 1–2, March 1997; Nataly Kelly, "Google Shakes Up the Translation Memory Scene," www.globalwatchtower.com, 8 August 2008; Vineeha Menon, "Google Takes Translation to the Next Level," www.itp.net/news, 6 August 2008; Sergei Nirenburg, "Knowledge Based Machine Translation," Machine Translation Journal, Springer, Netherlands, Volume 4 Number 1, March 1989; Franz Och, Christoph Tillman, Hermann Ney, "Improved Alignment Models for Statistical Machine Translation," http://www.aclweb.org/anthology-new/W/W99/W99-0604.pdf, 2005; Franz Och and H. Ney, "A Systematic Comparison of Various Statistical Alignment Models," *Computational Linguistics*, 29(1):19-51, 2003; Franz Och, Roy W. Tromble, Shankar Kumar, and Wolfgang Macherey, "Lattice Minimum Bayes-Risk Decoding for Statistical Machine Translation," Proceedings of the 2008 Conference on Empirical Methods in Natural Language Processing, pages 620–629, 2008; We-Yi Wang, Alex Waibel, "Decoding Algorithm in Statistical Machine Translation," Language Technology Institute paper.
[cxiii] OPEN Forum, 5 January 2010, http://www.openforum.com/idea-hub/topics/marketing/article/the-little-known-secret-to-getting-page-1-google-rankings-steve-strauss; theseomethod.com, accessed 11 Janu-

ary 2010, http://www.theseomethod.com/; websitehelpers.com, accessed 11 January 2010, http://websitehelpers.com/seo/blackhat.html; webworkshop.net, accessed 11 January 2010, http://www.webworkshop.net/seo-copywriting.html; seo.com, accessed 11 January 2010, http://www.webworkshop.net/seo-copywriting.html.

[cxiv] *Financial Times*, "How Gibes Could Counter Jihad," 16 April 2010.

[cxv] *CNN.com*, "In the Tech World, Porn Quietly Leads the Way," 23 April 2010, http://www.cnn.com/2010/TECH/04/23/porn.technology/index.html.

[cxvi] Ibid.

[cxvii] *The Jakarta Post*, "Former Jihad Members Get Lecture," 16 January 2006; Christopher Boucek, "Extremism Reeducation and Rehabilitation in Saudi Arabia," *Terrorism Monitor*, The Jamestown Foundation, Volume V, Issue 16, 16 August 2007.

[cxviii] P4Peace.com, accessed 30 November 2009, http://www.p4peace.com/subindex.asp?id=A122_09; *Straits Times*, 25 February 2009, http://www.straitstimes.com/Home.html; Alexa.com, accessed 2 December 2009, alexa.com.

AUTHOR'S BIOGRAPHY

Howard Gambrill Clark has dedicated his life to countering violent radicalization.

He graduated from Yale University with a degree in international relations focused on the Middle East. While a student, Mr. Clark was a writer for the State Department Public Diplomacy Washington File, Middle East/ South Asia division; served in the Senate Defense Appropriations Subcommittee; and studied Arabic at the American University in Cairo with a Department of Defense scholarship.

After Yale, Mr. Clark was a policy analyst in the Executive Office of the President for the President's Chief Economic Advisor.

Following the White House, Mr. Clark was commissioned in the U.S. Marine Corps. He completed two deployments to Iraq and one to the Philippines to combat insurgencies. In Iraq, he volunteered to command counter-terrorism document exploitation, reconnaissance, and human intelligence missions for various government agencies.

He then volunteered to be a combat replacement in Haditha where he led intelligence operations and wrote a key assessment on inspiring tribes to action. For intelligence excellence in Iraq, Mr. Clark received the Joint Commendation, Navy Commendation, and Navy Achievement Medals.

Upon release from the Marines, Mr. Clark was presidentially appointed to be Department of Homeland Security Chief Intelligence Officer Charles Allen's (who had 53 years of Intelligence Community experience) Special Assistant. For Mr. Allen, Mr. Clark drafted congressional testimonies and briefs. He also directed the preparation for President's Daily Brief terrorism sessions for Homeland Security.

Then, as Senior Intelligence Analyst for Homeland Security Counter Radicalization Branch, Mr. Clark helped lead the Intelligence Community in intelligence support for understanding counter-ideology. He published dozens of assessments for operators, Congress, the White House, and Cabinet to identify vulnerabilities in al-Qa'ida messaging and methods to strategically defeat al-Qa'ida marketing and worldwide growth. He was then promoted to Senior Intelligence Officer for Homeland Security Operations Intelligence Division.

Mr. Clark now advises government clients in creating counter-radicalization strategies in Southwest and Southeast Asia. Mr. Clark is also Founder and President of Seventh Pillar, Inc—a non-profit providing technical and educational support to community leaders around the world electing to counter al-Qa'ida's violent ideology and growth.

Mr. Clark resides in Washington, DC; Tampa, Florida; Paris, France; and Southwest Asia.